A HOLE IN THE HEAD

CARIB

A Hole in the Head

by

Arnold Schulman

Random House
New York

FIRST PRINTING

Photographs by courtesy of Ingeborg

Library of Congress Catalog Card Number: 57-11878

Manufactured in the United States of America

For Phyllis

A HOLE IN THE HEAD *was first presented by The Producers Theatre at the Plymouth Theatre, New York City, on February 28, 1957, with the following cast:*

(IN ORDER OF APPEARANCE)

FRANK	Milton J. Williams
TINA	Louise Erickson
MR. GOLDBLATT	Jacob Mestel
ALLY	Tommy White
MRS. FESSLER	Connie Sawyer
HERBERT	Larry Hart
MR. DIAMOND	Morris Strassberg
LENNY	Tom Pedi
SHIRL	Joyce Van Patten
SIDNEY	Paul Douglas
MAX	David Burns
SOPHIE	Kay Medford
MRS. ROGERS	Lee Grant

Directed by Garson Kanin
Production designed by Boris Aronson
Lighting by Jean Rosenthal
Costumes by Patton Campbell
Assistant to Mr. Kanin—Kip Good
Produced by Robert Whitehead

The action takes place at the Carabia, a small hotel in Miami Beach, Florida.

The time is the present.

PART ONE

Scene 1: Afternoon
Scene 2: One o'clock in the morning
Scene 3: Two hours later

PART TWO

Scene 1: That afternoon
Scene 2: That evening
Scene 3: The next morning

PART ONE

PART ONE

Scene 1

The Carabia, a small but ultramodern hotel on Ocean Drive, Miami Beach, Florida.

A hot sunny afternoon in the middle of July.

The set consists of two levels.

Stage right is a street leading to a small porch and to the lobby of the hotel. In the lobby are two modern upholstered swivel chairs, a small sofa and the hotel registration desk. Behind the desk is the switchboard, key rack, and an inner office with a door that leads off to the rear section of the hotel. Above the lobby is SHIRL'S *room, with bed, dressing table, and a small balcony. There is also a door leading into her dressing room and a front door which faces a flight of stairs down to the lobby.*

Stage left is the living room SIDNEY *shares with his son* ALLY. *It is divided from the lobby by the staircase and a hall leading to the rest of the hotel. The room has a small sofa, a desk, a very modern chair and a television set with a portable radio on top of it. At the back of the living room are two doors, one leading to the bedroom, the other to a clothes closet. Above the living room and directly across from* SHIRL'S *room is a sun deck with beach chairs.*

As the curtain rises, we hear music from SIDNEY'S *radio, and then a station break identifying the station as being in Miami.*

FRANK, *who is the combination bellboy-porter-relief desk clerk-*

switchboard operator and general all-around handy man, is at the moment doing none of these jobs. He is sprawled lazily in a chair on the porch, almost, but not quite, asleep.

The only other sign of life in the hotel is on the sun deck, where TINA, *a very well-proportioned young lady, is taking a sun bath.*

After a moment MR. GOLDBLATT *comes around the corner and up to the porch. He is a small man, in his seventies, dressed in a bright yellow terry-cloth robe and wearing a straw baseball-style cap. He is just coming from the beach.*

FRANK

Hi. How's the water?

MR. GOLDBLATT

Hot.

(*He continues into the lobby, then up the stairs toward his room, as* ALLY *appears, coming from behind the hotel.* ALLY *is almost twelve, but very short for his age and very skinny.*)

ALLY

Hi, Frank.

FRANK

Hi.

(ALLY *continues through the lobby to the living room, as* MRS. FESSLER *and* HERBERT *come around the corner and into the hotel.* MRS. FESSLER *is the epitome of the loving, solicitous mother.* HERBERT, *about eleven, has his arm in a sling.*)

ALLY

(*Calling into the bedroom*)

Pop? (MRS. FESSLER *and* HERBERT *go down the hall toward their room.* ALLY *turns off the radio, which had been left playing, then goes back to the lobby. Calls to* FRANK) Where's Pop?

(*He goes behind the registration desk.*)

FRANK

Beats me. (*Gets up, comes into the lobby toward* ALLY) Just told me to watch the board and took off.

ALLY

Any check-ins or anything?

FRANK

Check-ins? (*The very idea is absurd*) Ha. (ALLY *goes out to the back office as* MR. DIAMOND *comes up to the porch and sticks his head in the door. He is about sixty, a very nervous and gentle man. To* MR. DIAMOND) Not yet.

(MR. DIAMOND *makes a gesture of utter disgust and hopelessness, then turns and goes back off the porch and around the corner.*)

ALLY

(*Coming out*)

What?

FRANK

No, I was talking to What's-His-Name. The owner.

ALLY

(*This is bad news*)

Mr. Diamond?

FRANK

Now there is one nervous man what I call.

ALLY

What'd he say? Did he say anything?

FRANK

I don't know. They had an appointment. Something. Him and your dad. You going to stay a while? I'll get my coffee.

(*As* FRANK *starts out,* LENNY, *a tourist, comes down the hall and into the lobby. He is carrying a suitcase.*)

LENNY

(*To* ALLY, *behind the desk*)

What do I owe you? Four dollars? I'm checking out.

(FRANK *goes to him, reaches for the suitcase, but* LENNY *refuses to let* FRANK *have it.*)

ALLY

What's the matter? Something wrong, sir?

LENNY

Wrong? My brains. Ten thousand hotels in Miami Beach. My brains. I got to pick this one.

ALLY

If you don't like that room, sir . . .

LENNY

Like it? Sure. I love it. The bed's like iron, a hole in the pillowcase and no towels whatsoever. I like it fine. I mean, I been in a lot of hotels in my life, but no . . .

(SHIRL, *in her thirties, and magnificently constructed, comes up to the porch and into the lobby, and the sight of her instantly drives all other thoughts out of* LENNY'S *head. He stops, turns to stare at her as she comes toward the desk.*)

ALLY

(*To* FRANK)

Didn't the laundry come?

SHIRL

Hi, Frank.

LENNY

(*To* SHIRL)

Afternoon.

(*She withers him with a look.*)

FRANK

(*To* ALLY)

Well, the man came.

SHIRL

(*To* FRANK)

Mail in yet?

FRANK

Yes, ma'am.

ALLY

(*To* LENNY)

We've got plenty of towels.

SHIRL

Nothing?

FRANK

Not a thing.

SHIRL

For a change.

ALLY

(*Has taken this opportunity to pick up* LENNY's *bag and starts up the stairs with it*)

Let me give you a corner room, sir. We get twelve dollars a day for this room in the season.

LENNY

Will you give me that? (*He retrieves his suitcase, starts for the door, then stops beside* SHIRL) How about it, honey? Buy you a drink?

SHIRL

(*Striking out at him as if she were a cat*)

Psssssssstttttttttt!

LENNY

Pssssstt!

(*He goes out.* SHIRL *sits on the sofa.* ALLY *goes to the rack behind the desk and turns* LENNY'S *card up on end to signify a check-out.*)

ALLY

You see, Frank, if you don't get the whole week in advance? What happened to the laundry?

FRANK

The man wouldn't leave it till he gets paid first.

ALLY

Didn't you tell my dad he was here?

FRANK

How could I tell him?

ALLY

Boy.

FRANK

He's been gone all morning.

(*The switchboard buzzes.*)

ALLY

I'll get it, Frank. Get your coffee.

(ALLY *goes to the switchboard.*)

FRANK

(*To* SHIRL)

Bring you some coffee, ma'am?

SHIRL

(*The idea sounds repulsive to her*)

Akkk!

(FRANK *goes out.*)

ALLY

(*Into phone at switchboard*)

Order, please.

MR. GOLDBLATT'S VOICE

(*On the other end of the phone*)

Where's my towels?

ALLY

Didn't you get your towels?

MR. GOLDBLATT'S VOICE

It's terrible. I come in from the beach and find all dirty towels.

ALLY

I don't know how that happened, sir. I'll take care of it right away, sir.

(ALLY *goes into the back office.* SIDNEY *comes around the corner. He is about forty, a meticulous dresser, with a constant air of confidence and security. He carries a small package.*)

SIDNEY

(*Singing*)

"Love is a many splendored thing . . ." (*He stops suddenly at the lobby door when he sees* SHIRL. *She looks up, and for a mo-*

ment they stare at each other belligerently. To SHIRL, *as though he were saying "go to hell"*) How are you?

SHIRL

(*Just as hostilely*)

Why?

SIDNEY

Nothing.

(*He starts away from her, going behind the desk.*)

SHIRL

(*Calling after him, as though it were a dirty word*)

Landlord.

(SIDNEY, *behind the desk, automatically looks at the rack which shows which rooms are occupied and which are vacant.*)

ALLY

(*Comes out*)

Hi, Pop! Didn't we used to have some towels in the back?

SIDNEY

(*Referring to the upturned card in the rack*)

What'd that three-twelve check out?

ALLY

You know we don't have any clean towels?

SIDNEY

He just got here.

ALLY

The laundryman wouldn't leave the stuff till he gets paid first.

SIDNEY

How do you like that? Okay. That's all for them. You think that's the only laundry in town?

ALLY

I thought you paid them. Didn't you pay them?

SIDNEY

I'll pay them. What're they getting so worried about? Tell me. Who knocked out Rudy Zymeck? Newark, 1939.

ALLY

And that old man in five-oh-one just called.

SIDNEY

Come on. The second shortest fight on record.

ALLY

He's very mad about it.

SIDNEY

Will you answer the question?

ALLY

Alex Luke. Eleven seconds.

SIDNEY

Correct! For one million dollars.

ALLY

I'd better take him my towel. Okay? I didn't use it this morning.

SIDNEY

Will you let me take care of it? Now run outside and take a look at the car. I got a surprise for you.

ALLY

Will you take care of the old man?

SIDNEY

Hey, nag. You know you're a nag?

ALLY

I'm going.

(*He goes out.*)

SIDNEY

(*After a moment, to* SHIRL)

You mad?

SHIRL

What for?

SIDNEY

I don't know. You look mad.

SHIRL

At you?

SIDNEY

Just mad.

SHIRL

Know how you look?

SIDNEY

(*Smiles, comes to her. Turns on the little-boy charm*)

Miserable?

(SHIRL *looks at him for a moment, debating if she should forgive him or not.*)

SHIRL

(*Forgiving him*)

Want to see a monkey?

(*She holds her pocket mirror up to his face.*)

SIDNEY

Shirl, Shirl, honey . . .

ALLY

(*Calling from outside*)

What'd you do? Have it painted?

SIDNEY

(*Calling to* ALLY)

Like it? (*To* SHIRL) See you later?

ALLY

(*Coming in*)

What'd you do that for?

(SHIRL *goes upstairs to the sun deck.*)

SIDNEY

(*To* ALLY)

Well, I'll tell you. I bumped into my old friend, Moish. You know Honest Moish, the used-car dealer on Flagler, and we got to talking and . . . I don't know.

ALLY

You really get me.

SIDNEY

Don't you like it?

ALLY

We can't pay the laundry bill, we can't pay the rent, and you get the car painted. You know Mr. Diamond was here?

SIDNEY

You know you're a nag?

ALLY

What's he want?

SIDNEY

Who?

ALLY

His money?

SIDNEY

(Singing)

"Oh, love is a many splendored thing . . ."

ALLY

Pop?

SIDNEY

Hey, nag! What're you nagging all the time?

(FRANK *comes in with a container of coffee and a Danish.*)

FRANK

Hi. You back?

SIDNEY

What're you trying to do? Get fat there?

(*He breaks off a piece of* FRANK'S *Danish and begins eating it.*)

FRANK

Did Ally tell you?

SIDNEY

Yeah.

FRANK

Mr. What's-His-Name . . .

ALLY

Diamond.

FRANK

. . . was here.

SIDNEY

I know.

FRANK

Said you had an appointment.

SIDNEY

I know.

FRANK

At three o'clock.

SIDNEY

I know!

ALLY

(*To* FRANK)

In case the old man calls again, his towel's on the way.

(ALLY *goes to his bedroom, comes out in an instant with a towel, then takes the towel up the stairs.*)

SIDNEY

(*Opening the mail*)

Bills. Bills. Everything's a bill. Look at a nice little envelope, you think it's a letter something. Reservation. No. They disguise it on you. (*Turns to* FRANK) What'd he seem, mad, Diamond?

FRANK

What?

SIDNEY

Listen, get me person-to-person my brother Max in New York.

(SIDNEY *takes his package and goes to his room, where he unwraps the package and takes out two loud, but smart, sports shirts. He turns on the radio.* FRANK *finds the number in the personal address book on the switchboard and starts the call as* MR. DIAMOND *comes to the porch, then into the lobby to the desk.*)

FRANK

(*Into the phone*)

Hello, this is the Carabia. Jefferson two, one-oh-one-oh calling person-to-person in New York Mr. Max Young at Fordham three, nine-oh-two-nine. Time and charges please.

MR. DIAMOND

Excuse me. You know where I can reach him maybe on the telephone?

FRANK

Hi! He just came in. (*Calling in to* SIDNEY) Mr. Diamond's here.

SIDNEY

(*Comes to meet him*)

Hi ya, boy? How's the boy?

MR. DIAMOND

I was here three o'clock.

SIDNEY

Yeah. I'm sorry. I got tied up. (*He realizes he has one of the shirts in his hand*) You like these?

MR. DIAMOND

For me or for you?

SIDNEY

Listen. It wouldn't kill you to wear a little color. Look the way you dress. A rich man like you.

MR. DIAMOND

Rich.

SIDNEY

Listen. If I had your money . . . Sit down. What're you standing?

MR. DIAMOND

Tell me, Sidney. You got it?

SIDNEY

I'll get it.

MR. DIAMOND

You'll get it is one thing. You got it?

SIDNEY

Listen. It takes a little time. Can I pick up five grand in the street?

MR. DIAMOND

Sidney, don't make me out a mean man. I'm not a mean man. I gave you three months. You know another man in business wouldn't close you right up?

SIDNEY

Don't give me the pressure, boy.

MR. DIAMOND

I won't give you the pressure. Give me the money.

SIDNEY

Wait till the season. Nobody pays rent in the summertime.

MR. DIAMOND

Sidney, please. I know you a long time. I knew your wife, may she rest in peace. Your boy is like my own flesh and blood. You think I want to throw you out? Three months I waited like a gentleman. My wife's beginning to holler.

SIDNEY

Listen. I can't meet a payment, you're going to throw me out in the street?

(ALLY *comes down stairs from* MR. GOLDBLATT'S *room and sits at the edge of the lobby.*)

MR. DIAMOND

You got a lease? What's it say in the lease?

SIDNEY

Don't tell me leases.

MR. DIAMOND

You want to play marbles, play marbles. I'm a businessman. You want to do business, don't play marbles.

SIDNEY

You'll get your money. Don't worry.

MR. DIAMOND

This week?

SIDNEY

This week. This week.

MR. DIAMOND

I'm not a mean man. You signed it yourself in the lease.

SIDNEY

Mean? You're a crumb. I don't mind telling you.

MR. DIAMOND

Is that nice?

SIDNEY

Frank, you put that call in?

FRANK

The line's busy. They're going to call right back.

SIDNEY

Stick around. I got a call in to my brother. I want you to hear this. He'll give me the money in a minute.

MR. DIAMOND

Good. I'll be tickled to death.

SIDNEY

Just stick around.

MR. DIAMOND

I don't have to hear it.

SIDNEY

Crumb.

MR. DIAMOND

You don't pay the rent and I'm the crumb.

(He goes out. There is a long pause. SIDNEY *goes to his*

room. ALLY *follows him, turning off the radio when he comes into the room.*)

SIDNEY

Would you believe a man could be like that?

ALLY

He's right, you know.

SIDNEY

What right? What do you know? Right.

ALLY

It says in the lease you don't meet the payment, you lose the security.

(SHIRL *leaves the sun deck and goes into her room.*)

SIDNEY

What do you know? What do you know so much?

ALLY

I took it out last night and read through it.

SIDNEY

What you took?

(*The switchboard buzzes.*)

ALLY

The lease.

SIDNEY

I told you to stay out of that drawer. Didn't I tell you? (*The phone rings.* SIDNEY *picks up phone*) Hello, Max? That you, Max? Sidney. How are you, Max?

(*He chases* ALLY *out of the room, but* ALLY *stands outside the door, listening.*)

MAX'S VOICE

Sidney?

SIDNEY

How's Sophie?

MAX'S VOICE

Terrible. What do you want?

SIDNEY

No kidding. That's a shame. Everybody's getting it lately. Like a virus.

MAX'S VOICE

What?

SIDNEY

A virus.

MAX'S VOICE

What?

SIDNEY

Like a virus.

MAX'S VOICE

What do you mean virus? She don't feel good.

SIDNEY

I don't know. In the old days you had a cold. Now everything's a virus. Listen, Max. I'll tell you why I called.

MAX'S VOICE

Why I know. How much?

SIDNEY

What do you mean, how much? I think you know me too good. Huh, Max? Can you hear me all right?

MAX'S VOICE

I hear you. I hear you. That's the whole trouble. I hear you too good. How much do you need?

SIDNEY

Fifty-three hundred dollars. (*Silence*) Hello? Max? You still there?

MAX'S VOICE

Fifty-three hundred dollars?

SIDNEY

I got nervous. I thought you hung up.

MAX'S VOICE

Fifty-three hundred dollars?

SIDNEY

Max . . .

MAX'S VOICE

Fifty-three hundred dollars?

SIDNEY

Don't get excited.

MAX'S VOICE

What do you think, I'm a bank? Go to the bank.

SIDNEY

I tried the banks. Everything. Would I ask you if I wasn't in a box? They're going to take away the whole place and everything. They're going to put me out on the street and I got all that money tied up.

MAX'S VOICE

Fifty-three hundred dollars.

SIDNEY

The security. Every penny I got in this world. You know I wouldn't ask you for myself. But the kid, he needs a lot of special care now.

MAX'S VOICE

What's the matter, he's sick?

SIDNEY

I don't want to talk about it. How's Sophie?

MAX'S VOICE

Sidney. I'm your brother. If the boy is sick . . .

SIDNEY

It's not too serious. I think we caught it in time.

MAX'S VOICE

What's the doctor say?

SIDNEY

They don't know.

MAX'S VOICE

They don't know?

SIDNEY

They can't tell.

MAX'S VOICE

That's very bad.

SIDNEY

Like stomach trouble. He's got stomach trouble.

(SHIRL *goes to her balcony, sits and works on a crossword puzzle.*)

MAX'S VOICE

Terrible. Terrible.

SIDNEY

Doctors. You know. First they take your money, then they don't know.

MAX'S VOICE

A terrible thing.

SIDNEY

Max, I don't want you to tell Sophie about this. Will you promise me? I don't want her to get worried.

MAX'S VOICE

Terrible.

SIDNEY

And don't you worry about anything. I'll find the money some place.

MAX'S VOICE

Sidney. Are you telling me the truth?

SIDNEY

Are you kidding me? You're going to make me very mad in a minute. Did I ever lie to you?

MAX'S VOICE

Yes.

SIDNEY

When did I ever lie to you?

MAX'S VOICE

When?

SIDNEY

You think I'd lie about a thing like that?

MAX'S VOICE

I'm telling you, Sidney.

SIDNEY

Listen.

MAX'S VOICE

If you're lying to me . . .

SIDNEY

Forget it.

MAX'S VOICE

All right. I'll think it over.

SIDNEY

There's nothing to think over. If you send me a check I'll tear it up. I mean it. I should drop dead on this spot . . . Max? . . . Hello?

(*He hangs up, pleased with the way it turned out.* ALLY *comes into the room with a book.*)

ALLY

Boy.

SIDNEY

What "boy"?

ALLY

You really get me.

SIDNEY

What're you, starting again?

ALLY

Who's got stomach trouble?

SIDNEY

All of a sudden you never had a bellyache in your life?

ALLY

You didn't say bellyache.

SIDNEY

Sunday you had it. Thursday you had it. Every time I look around you got a bellyache.

ALLY

One time. That's all. That fried salami. That don't mean I've got stomach trouble.

(MRS. FESSLER *comes through the hall and goes out around the corner.*)

SIDNEY

Listen, big shot. Can I tell you something? When you don't understand something keep your mouth shut on the subject. That's the whole thing I want to tell you.

ALLY

What subject?

SIDNEY

You don't understand a thing how business works. What're you, George Washington? Suppose I run an ad, what should I advertise? No towels? You exaggerate a little. Ocean front. Solarium. Air conditioning. What's the difference you got it or not? They come in, you'll play it by ear. You know? People are used to it.

ALLY

I'm not.

SIDNEY

You. Big shot. Whatever anything is, that's what you hate. I guarantee you tomorrow morning we'll have a check from your Uncle Max. Bet? He's just got to talk it over with Sophie first.

ALLY

Well, that takes care of that.

SIDNEY

How do you know so much? What're you, some kind of gypsy? Even Max don't know yet he's going to give me the money, so how do you know so much? So mind your own business—you hear me? You talk too much.

ALLY

I hear you.

(*Pause, then* SIDNEY *goes to him.*)

SIDNEY

What's the matter? You mad? (ALLY *doesn't look at him.* SIDNEY *turns on the radio*) Look at the crazy books he reads. All about anything.

ALLY

It's a science book.

SIDNEY

No kidding. What do you call them things? Dinoserouses?

ALLY

Dinosaurs.

SIDNEY

Big deal. What do you read so much? Want to ruin your eyes? (*There is a pause*) I told you I'm sorry.

ALLY

When?

SIDNEY

Didn't I tell you?

ALLY

I talk too much.

SIDNEY

Who said you talk too much?

ALLY

You did.

SIDNEY

Listen. You talk. Don't listen to anybody. You want to talk? You talk. (*Looking through the book as he sits on sofa*) What'd they, make a picture out of this book?

ALLY

It's a science book.

SIDNEY

What do I care? I seen this picture they made with this guy . . . What's his name? . . . He's got black hair. You know who I mean. And he was a caveman like in the picture and they had all these animals like running around. So don't look at me I'm stupid.

ALLY

(*Sitting next to* SIDNEY)

Pop?

SIDNEY

What?

ALLY

I want to stay here with you.

SIDNEY

What're you talking?

ALLY

She mentioned it once, Aunt Sophie. Don't you remember? Right after Mama died, how you can't take care of me and all that, and a boy like me and everything needs a decent home and all that. You remember.

SIDNEY

You got a decent home?

ALLY

Sure.

SIDNEY

So what're you worried about?

ALLY

I know it's decent and you know it's decent but does Uncle Max know it's decent?

SIDNEY

Will you listen to me? Anybody tries to take you away from me is in for a potful of trouble, and I don't mean maybe. Look at me. Look in my face. You believe me?

ALLY

I believe you.

SIDNEY

Then how come you look so worried?

ALLY

That's just the way I look. I've got that kind of face. I don't know.

SIDNEY

(*Poking* ALLY)

Listen. What do you say we take a ride. Okay? Want to take a ride?

ALLY

(*Laughs*)

You really get me.

SIDNEY

What're you laughing?

ALLY

Is that all we gotta do?

SIDNEY

Victor Mature.

ALLY

What?

SIDNEY

In that picture. He was this caveman and they lived in a cave.

ALLY

Boy.

SIDNEY

What a lousy picture.

ALLY

Will you tell me something?

SIDNEY

What?

ALLY

Who was the first light-heavyweight to hold three crowns?

SIDNEY

For one millon dollars?

ALLY

For one million dollars.

(SIDNEY *and* ALLY *embrace, holding each other tightly, warmly.*)

SIDNEY

Don't be crazy. There's nobody in this world can take you away from me.

Dimout

In the darkness we hear the radio. There is a station break giving the time of day and the weather forecast.

Scene 2

One o'clock in the morning.

TINA *is on the sun deck in the moonlight. As she lights a cigarette, the lights come up, revealing* ALLY *and* SIDNEY *in their room.* SIDNEY *has nearly fallen asleep on the chair while looking at the* Ring *magazine.* ALLY, *however, has managed to keep him awake for some time now.*

The radio is playing jazz. There is a long pause.

ALLY

Pop? (SIDNEY *grunts*) Can I see that telegram again?

SIDNEY

No.

ALLY

Why not?

SIDNEY

I'm sleeping.

ALLY

I just want to look at it.

SIDNEY

Will you leave me alone?

ALLY

It takes about forty-five minutes to get out to the airport and if you run into some traffic . . .

SIDNEY

Hey, nag-o. Will you stop nagging? Ooooh! What a nag! (SHIRL *comes into her room from her dressing room. She paces.*)

ALLY

If the plane gets in at two o'clock you ought to leave right now. That's all I'm going to say about it.

SIDNEY

Good. That's all? Fine.

ALLY

I mean it. (*There is a pause*) Pop?

SIDNEY

I'm going to floor you.

ALLY

Don't you think it's funny Uncle Max gets on an airplane and comes down here just like that?

SIDNEY

Why don't you go eat? Did you eat supper?

ALLY

I'll eat.

SIDNEY

It's one o'clock in the morning. When you going to eat your supper? For breakfast?

ALLY

You don't think Aunt Sophie is coming with him, do you?

SIDNEY

How can she come? Who's going to watch the store?

ALLY

I sure hope not.

SIDNEY

Very nice. You got a lot of respect for your family.

ALLY

Well, she's the one started all that talk before. About how you can't take care of me, and I ought to have a decent home and all that.

SIDNEY

You starting up again?

ALLY

I'm just telling you.

SIDNEY

It's a simple business proposition. That's all. Before he puts five grand in the place he wants to have a look at it. Is that a terrible crime? No. You got to make a whole federal case out of it. Now go out and get something to eat, and I mean it. You think I want your Uncle Max to see you looking so skinny?

ALLY

(*He goes to the door, stops, turns around*)

Pop?

SIDNEY

I'm going to floor you!

ALLY

I'm going!

(*As he goes out, he turns the radio off.* SIDNEY *sits for a moment, chuckling to himself, then he gets up, picks out a sports coat, and goes out, automatically turning the radio back on. He goes to the porch, stops, is tempted to go up to* SHIRL's *room, resists the temptation for just a moment, but finally goes up to her door. The door is open slightly to get a draft into the room. She is seated at the dressing table. He knocks on the door and opens it at the same time.*)

SIDNEY

(*Just sticking his head in*)

Hi.

SHIRL

Hi.

SIDNEY

I made up my mind not to see you tonight.

SHIRL

So?

SIDNEY

I got to go out to the airport.

SHIRL

I know. You told me.

SIDNEY

I know I told you.

SHIRL

Either come in or go out. You make me nervous.

(SIDNEY *comes in, stands for a while, looking out the window onto her balcony. She continues brushing her hair.*)

SIDNEY

Man, oh, man. How I'd love to pick up, me and you, and take off. I don't know. Africa. Some place. Let the wind blow.

SHIRL

I can pack in five minutes.

SIDNEY

Would you?

SHIRL

What have I got to lose?

SIDNEY

You'd go with me?

SHIRL

I go where the kicks are, and when the kicks stop coming—

SIDNEY

You take off?

SHIRL

Like a greased bird.

SIDNEY

That's what bothers me.

SHIRL

You blame me?

SIDNEY

I don't blame you. It just bothers me.

SHIRL

Why?

SIDNEY

You can't rent all your rooms every night.

SHIRL

Maybe *you* can't.

SIDNEY

(*Starts to laugh to himself*)

You want to know what I'm laughing? I'm just thinking. My brother Max ever seen me and you together. That's the end of that.

SHIRL

Who's your brother? A bear? What're you scared about? Let him bark.

SIDNEY

I want to clue you. Bears don't bark. Dogs bark. A bear don't say nothing.

SHIRL

What'm I, going to fight with you about bears?

SIDNEY

I seen a couple bears already. Where my brother Max used to live in North Carolina they used to walk around on the streets there. I'm not kidding. In the mountains there.

SHIRL

Good. That makes you an expert on bears.

SIDNEY

Just don't talk about what you never seen. I seen a couple of bears already. They got a bear up there lives in a cave. You bring him a bottle of beer or something, he drinks it right in front of you. (*He looks at her for a moment*) Shirl, I'm not scared of my brother. I mean it. Listen. I'm going to ask him for money. He thinks I'm a goof as it is. You don't know this guy. Most old-fashioned man you ever seen. He thinks any girl's a blonde is no good. Just like that. He thinks I ought to live in a cave some place like a monk some place. You don't know this guy. I mean it. You know his idea of a big time? Penny ante in the kitchen. Not even for money yet. For matches.

SHIRL

You should have known my husband.

SIDNEY

Listen.

SHIRL

The same way. All they want to do is sit around in a deep hole some place. You talk about fun they yell bloody murder you said a dirty word.

SIDNEY

That's him. That's my brother.

SHIRL

That's all of them.

SIDNEY

Shirl, Shirl, honey . . .
(*They kiss.*)

SHIRL

You better go if you're going.

SIDNEY

I know. (*He forces himself to move away from her, but still is unable to leave the room*) Nineteen forty-six. Know how much money I was worth? Two hundred thousand dollars, on paper. Know how much I got now? Just about enough to take us to the outskirts of town.

SHIRL

And if you had money?

SIDNEY

What do you mean?

SHIRL

You'd just pick up and take off? Just like that?

SIDNEY

Sure I would.

SHIRL

And the kid?

SIDNEY

Listen . . .

SHIRL

You talk. Hooray. Let's get in that big red car and take off through the woods, but inside, not you, landlord. You know your trouble? You're not selfish enough.

SIDNEY

Me? I'm the most selfish guy in the world.

SHIRL

Would you leave your kid? (SIDNEY *turns away*) That's what I like about you.

SIDNEY

What's to like? You know? I could touch a piece of solid gold. Pssssst. Spaghetti, right in front of my eyes.

SHIRL

Know why? You've got your face down. That's why.

SIDNEY

I don't want to look at you.

SHIRL

Hello.

SIDNEY

Please. Don't look in my face.

SHIRL

Don't you think *I* want to cry?

SIDNEY

What do you want to cry for? No worries. Free. A wild bird. The whole world to fly in.

SHIRL

Sure. I'm a bird, all right.

SIDNEY

But you're not, are you?

SHIRL

Am I?

SIDNEY

What's the matter with us? I've known a million women in my life. Shirl, do we have to go on killing each other? I always

have to hurt you or you hurt me. It's crazy. Are you my enemy I've got to cut you up in little pieces? (*He lies down next to* SHIRL *on the bed*) Shirl, tell me. What's the matter with us?

SHIRL

You've got to go.

SIDNEY

I know.

SHIRL

It's getting late.

SIDNEY

I know.

SHIRL

I don't want to hurt you.

SIDNEY

Shirl . . . maybe some day, maybe I will, Shirl. I'll find the kid a decent home and . . . listen, Shirl . . .

SHIRL

You've got to go!

SIDNEY

I want you, Shirl. I need you, Shirl. I want you all the time.

SHIRL

I don't want that.

SIDNEY

Shirl . . .

SHIRL

Not always.

SIDNEY

Please!

SHIRL

I just want you now.

(*They kiss.*)

Dimout

In the darkness we hear a radio commercial about refrigerators and how your kitchen space problem can be solved.

Scene 3

About two-thirty in the morning.

In the dark a match is struck on the sun deck. We see TINA *lighting a cigarette.*

Then another match is struck on the sun deck. We see a young man sitting a few feet away from her. He lights a cigarette. Watches TINA.

The lights come up on the set below them.

Except for a small night light in the lobby, the only other light in the hotel is in SIDNEY'S *room, where* ALLY *is alone, having fallen asleep on the sofa, his book beside him.*

SIDNEY *is asleep on* SHIRL'S *bed.*

After a moment MAX *comes in. He stops in the lobby, puts his suitcase down, looks around, then* SOPHIE *comes in.*

MAX *is in his late fifties. A very nervous man. A realist. An ultraconservative.*

SOPHIE, *his wife, is sweet and sentimental, but rules her household with an iron hand.*

SOPHIE

So where is everybody?

MAX

It's two o'clock in the morning.

SOPHIE

I mean Sidney. Ally. Somebody.

MAX

Maybe he didn't get the telegram.

SOPHIE

Max? . . . Maybe he's at the hospital.

MAX

Hospital.

SOPHIE

So how come he didn't come out the airport to meet us?

MAX

If I could give you a reason would I give you a reason?

SOPHIE

I just have a feeling, don't ask me why, that boy is in the hospital, and you know who I hold responsible? You.

MAX

Thank you.

SOPHIE

He's always been a sick little boy and I told you, Max. You know I told you. That Sidney cannot take care of a little boy. All right. Now you're satisfied? I just hope, please God, it's not too serious.

MAX

He said the boy had a little stomach ache. What am I doing here? All of a sudden I look around, you got me on an airplane.

SOPHIE

Max. Look in the phone book, you'll call up all the hospitals.

MAX

I'm not going to call the hospitals. You're making me crazy.

SOPHIE

Maybe they got a clerk in the back fell asleep.

MAX

(*Sees the bell on the desk, starts ringing it*)
Who's here? Is anybody here?

SOPHIE

Max! Shh. Max.

MAX

(*Still ringing the bell*)
Is anybody here?

(*Suddenly a light snaps on in* SHIRL'S *room.* SIDNEY, *apparently awakened out of a deep sleep, has turned on the bed lamp.*)

SOPHIE

Will you stop that? You want to wake up the whole town?

MAX

What am I going to do? Stand here?

(ALLY, *hearing the bell, starts putting on his shoes, so he can go out to the lobby.*)

SIDNEY

(Looking at his watch)

My God! Will you look what time it is?

(He grabs his clothes and goes into the bathroom. ALLY *comes out to the lobby.)*

ALLY

Yes, sir. Can I . . . Uncle Max!

*(*MAX *stands still for a long moment. He looks at* SOPHIE, *then he turns back to* ALLY.*)*

MAX

So when'd you get out of the hospital?

SOPHIE

What're you doing up?

ALLY

Where's Dad? He went out to meet you.

MAX

(To SOPHIE*)*

I won't say nothing.

SOPHIE

Ally. You all right?

ALLY

I'm fine.

SOPHIE

You had me worried to death.

MAX

Not a word.

SOPHIE

Your daddy told us you're sick. We rushed right down here . . .

ALLY

Well, I was a little bit.

SOPHIE

(*To* MAX)

Look how pale he looks.

ALLY

It wasn't anything serious.

SOPHIE

Let me feel your head. You got a fever?

ALLY

I just had a little upset stomach, but I'm okay now. Honest.

MAX

You know how much it costs to go on the airplane? Over two hundred dollars. Two hundred dollars. I've got to leave my store . . . I'm not going to say anything . . .

SOPHIE

You should thank God the boy's all right. What're you talking, two hundred dollars? You mad he's not sick? I'm only thankful the boy is . . . (*She holds him*) Ally . . . Ally, I'm so happy. You had me worried to death. Let me sit down. Look at my heart. It's beating.

(*She sits down on the sofa.*)

ALLY

I know he went to meet you.

SOPHIE

That Sidney. He did it again. I thought I would never live to see the day I would believe a word that man told me, but look at me. I'm sitting here in Florida. All right. It's a good thing we came down. At least we know. That Sidney.

MAX

It's so funny. Six o'clock I'm sitting in my own kitchen having supper and now I could look around and see a coconut.

SOPHIE

When I told him airplane he looked at me.

MAX

Uh. Look at the big hero there. She told me airplane. The woman comes around says put the strap on. I looked out the window. Fire is coming on the motors there. I look at Sophie. She's white?

SOPHIE

I was not.

MAX

Like a pillowcase.

SOPHIE

What's to be scared about?

MAX

I'll tell you the truth. It's very nice when you think about it. Four hours. Would you believe it? On the train right now we're in Baltimore some place and my underwear is just beginning to crawl up on me.

SOPHIE

Max!

MAX

What'd I say! Underwear?

ALLY

You want to wash up or something? Let me show you your room.

MAX

We'll wait a few minutes. Maybe Sidney'll be here.

SOPHIE

What do you think, Max? We'll go home tomorrow?

MAX

What then? A vacation? In the middle of nothing?

SOPHIE

I thought maybe as long as we're down here.

MAX

If I had somebody in the store . . .

SOPHIE

Albert's in the store.

MAX

Albert.

SOPHIE

Your own son. You talk about him like . . . I don't know what.

MAX

In the house he's my son, in the store—he's a tumor.

SOPHIE

All right. I'll call Mrs. Rogers in the morning, and maybe in the afternoon we can see the Feldmans a few minutes.

MAX

Personally, I could live without Mrs. Rogers and the Feldmans together.

SOPHIE

If we leave at night we'll be home in the morning. We don't have to break our necks.

MAX

You know what I could use? A soda.

SOPHIE

Now you want a soda? You'll be up half the night.

ALLY

I'll go in the back and get us some.

MAX

Naw. She's right. I drink too much soda. That's how come I got all that gas in my system.

SOPHIE

You go to bed, Ally. You don't have to wait up like this. Look how bad he looks. Tell me. What did you eat today? Tell me everything you ate. Start with breakfast. Did you drink milk?

ALLY

Well, frankly, I'm not too crazy about milk.

MAX

He's a good boy. We'll take him home . . . (*He pinches* ALLY's *arm affectionately*) in two weeks he'll be a different person. Fat. A little color in his face . . .

SOPHIE

Would you like that, Ally?

ALLY

Ma'am?

SOPHIE

That's the only reason we came down here, to see if you'd

come live with us. We've got a big house and nobody left to enjoy it. The boys are both gone and me and your Uncle Max, we live in one room, the kitchen.

ALLY

Well, gee . . . I'd like to . . . but you know . . . I mean . . . you know . . .

SOPHIE

It would be so nice to have a little noise in the house again. You know, we have two bicycles in our house? Left over from when our boys were little.

MAX

What bicycles? You kept those bicycles?

SOPHIE

Sure I kept them, and now you see they come in handy. So don't tell me all the time throw out, throw out.

MAX

Everything she keeps..

SOPHIE

You like to ride a bicycle?

ALLY

Well, not too much. I mean it's all right, but you know.

MAX

(*Who has become entwined in a very modern chair*)

I don't know. I can't seem to get comfortable. You ever seen a chair like this in your life? What kind of crazy chair to have around a place?

ALLY

Why don't we go inside our room and wait?

MAX

What do you want to do, Sophie? You want to wait or go to bed?

SOPHIE

All right. Five minutes. He don't come we'll go to bed. (ALLY *takes them to his room.* SOPHIE *looks around*) This is the whole place?

ALLY

Oh, no. We've got this other room, in here, where we sleep.

MAX

(*Sitting down*)

You know what hurts? My feet hurt. One of these days I'll buy some arch supporters. I hear they're very nice.

(MRS. FESSLER *comes into the lobby. She is gloriously drunk. She makes her way to the desk, takes her key and exits through the hall, very, very happy. On the sun deck the man starts talking to* TINA. *In* SHIRL'S *room,* SID *kisses* SHIRL *and then comes down to his room. He is smeared with lipstick.*)

SIDNEY

Max! Sophie! When'd you get here? I looked all over the airport for you. What happened? You couldn't wait two minutes till I got there? I looked from one end of the place to the other. (*He goes to* SOPHIE, *hugs her*) How are you, beautiful? How's your virus? (SOPHIE *pushes him away. She looks at his face to confirm what she suspects, then, verifying her suspicion, she takes his pocket handkerchief and wipes some lipstick from his face. She shows the handkerchief to* MAX. *Upstairs,* SHIRL *goes to bed*) What? What're you doing? Listen. You think? . . . I met a friend of mine out the airport. Some old woman, I know her a hundred years. What're you, crazy?

MAX

That Sidney. Well, Sidney, you didn't change. Huh, Sidney?

SIDNEY

Ally, did you take your medicine, go take your medicine—stomach trouble.

SOPHIE

Stomach trouble.

MAX

Stomach trouble. You're looking good, Sidney. Like a doctor. Look how he looks like a doctor.

SOPHIE

Very nice.

MAX

That Sidney. He could wear a tuxedo. Like a regular doctor. (SIDNEY *laughs nervously*) Everything he laughs, Sidney. I should have your worries. Look how he laughs at everything. You ever worry a day in your life, Sidney? Tell the truth. That's a Sidney, boy? Some Sidney.

SIDNEY

(*Opening closet door and hanging up his jacket*)

What do you mean? I worry plenty.

MAX

He worries.

SOPHIE

(*Looking in the closet*)

Look, Max. Look at all the suits.

SIDNEY

You like them? I got me a tailor down the street. He makes them to order for me.

MAX

How much they cost you?

SIDNEY

Well . . . they don't cost much.

MAX

A hundred dollars? I bet they cost a hundred dollars apiece.

SIDNEY

I got to do it, Max. I can't get nothing in the store to fit me. I'm built all wrong.

SOPHIE

You see, Max? You get to be a big hotel man in Miami you can wear hundred-dollar suits.

SIDNEY

(*Tries to ease the tension with humor*)

Look at them, standing there, you two. You got it all wrong—these ain't my suits, they're Ally's. (*Puts jacket on* ALLY) He lost a little weight—stomach trouble. How do you like this kid—we can't pay the rent, we can't pay the laundry bill, and you buy hundred-dollar suits!

(*He laughs, and, in spite of themselves,* MAX *and* SOPHIE *laugh too.*)

SOPHIE

How could anybody hate you, Sidney?

MAX

That's a Sidney in America?

SOPHIE

If only you would act like a human being. We like you, Sidney, but you act so crazy.

SIDNEY

That's my nature. Sue me.

(*He kisses* SOPHIE *on the neck.*)

SOPHIE

I'm serious.

SIDNEY

Listen. I want to make one suggestion. I know you're both

tired. It's a long trip. Why don't you go to bed, get a good night's sleep. Get up late in the morning. You know? You'll spend the whole day on the beach and I'll take you out tomorrow to a wonderful dinner. All right? We've got plenty of time to talk. As long as you're down here you might as well take it easy. Enjoy yourself.

MAX

Sidney, I'll tell you the truth, we've been doing a lot of thinking. I don't have to tell you business today is not one hundred percent perfect. In my store . . .

SIDNEY

Don't cry, Max. You're always crying with a loaf of bread in your hand. You got something to say, say it.

MAX

Sidney, the last time I was down here I looked around the place. I looked up and down the street. The whole neighborhood. It's no good, Sidney. All the business has moved already. Who's going to stay here? They've got such beautiful hotels up there in the best section now, for the same money why should they stop here? And I told you then, Sidney. Get rid of the place. Did I tell you?

SIDNEY

You won't give me the money. Right?

MAX

You want me to throw good money in the ash can?

SIDNEY

Okay. Forget it. You want to be like that? Fine.

MAX

Like what?

SIDNEY

I'm your brother.

MAX

What do I owe you?

(SOPHIE *grabs* ALLY *and rushes him toward the bedroom so that he will not witness the imminent fight.*)

SIDNEY

Forget it.

MAX

Do I owe you something?

SOPHIE

Don't get excited.

MAX

What do I owe him?

SIDNEY

Forget it. Who needs you?

MAX

Go in your big car, big shot.

SIDNEY

All of a sudden . . .

MAX

The big shot.

SIDNEY

. . . I'm going to run away with his money.

MAX

I don't have a Packard car. I don't go around with all kinds of tramps to a night club. I have a Chevrolet. Ten years I got it. It takes me where I want to go. It runs good. I don't have a Packard car. You bum.

SIDNEY

Bum!

MAX

You know why it runs good? I take care of it.

SIDNEY

Who's talking about cars?

MAX

Hundred-dollar suits.

SIDNEY

You crazy?

(SOPHIE *emerges from the bedroom and tries to "shush" them, then returns to the bedroom.* MAX *and* SIDNEY *glare at each other—each daring the other to speak. Finally* SIDNEY *walks to the radio and turns it on.* MAX *goes over to the desk and looks out the window There is a long pause.*)

MAX

(*Unable to hold it in another second*)

In your whole life you ever sat still? Running, here, there. How many stores you had in your life? How many times you come to me for help? Ha? Ha? It's about time you stood on your own two feet. No more, Sidney. Nobody in the family. Before we left I called the whole family on the telephone and we talked it over and everybody said the same thing. The trouble is we've been too good to you. All you have to do is run around with girls. Who knows what? You need money? The family. Only no more, Sidney. (SOPHIE *comes out of the bedroom*) Nothing. Not a penny.

SIDNEY

Fine. Good. Who needs you? Good-bye and good luck.

MAX

Bum.

SOPHIE

Max.

SIDNEY

Bum?

SOPHIE

Max! Sidney! You want to wake up the whole building?

There's something more important we've got to talk about and there's no reason we can't sit down like human beings. Sit down, Max! Sidney, please. (SOPHIE *turns off the radio.* MAX *and* SIDNEY *reluctantly sit*) Sidney, I want you to think about this before you say no right away.

SIDNEY

Listen, Sophie.

SOPHIE

Will you let me talk? We want to do the right thing, that's all. We don't want to hurt anybody, but we thought about it a lot and what's right is right, and that's how come we came down here.

SIDNEY

Sophie, don't say what you're going to say. I don't want to hear it.

MAX

What do you think? We're going to let the boy live here like this?

SIDNEY

You can't take my kid away.

MAX

Tell me, Sidney. How much money you got in the bank?

SIDNEY

That's none of your business.

MAX

You got enough to pay your rent?

SIDNEY

I'll pay it.

MAX

You got enough to open up another business some place when they throw you out of here?

SIDNEY

Don't worry about it.

MAX

I'm asking you.

SOPHIE

What are you going to do without money?

MAX

This hotel you can forget about. I wouldn't give you a dime.

SOPHIE

Think about it, Sidney. What can you do to make a living? Can you find a steady job some place?

MAX

Sidney? He couldn't work for anybody his life depended on it.

SOPHIE

Can you hammer a nail, plant a seed, make a dress? What can you do to make a living?

SIDNEY

Listen. I might of borrowed a few dollars once in a while . . .

SOPHIE

Sidney . . .

SIDNEY

But I never went hungry. I could go on the road tomorrow and knock down two, three hundred a week.

SOPHIE

That's exactly what we're talking about. We know you can make a living, but how? What can you do? There's only three things you ever did in your life. You had a store, which you hate and anyhow you don't have the money to open one right now. You ran a hotel, which you can't do any more because you don't have any money. And you were a salesman on the road. Am I right, Sidney?

SIDNEY

Wait a minute. Listen. I want to tell you about the hotel.

MAX

Forget the hotel.

SIDNEY

They got all my money. That security. I got a lot of money in this place.

MAX

If you'd watch your business instead of running around so much . . .

SIDNEY

(*Rising*)

What am I going to watch? You want me to chase people in off the streets?

SOPHIE

Will you stop it? Both of you. Sit down, Max. (*He does*) The point is this, Sidney. You have to go on the road and be a salesman. There's nothing else you can do, and while you're away on the road who's going to take care of the boy? Who's going to cook his meals and wash his clothes and see he don't get sick? Who? Tell me who?

MAX

You want him to be a bum like you?

SIDNEY

Bum?

MAX

Bum. Bum.

SIDNEY

I told you. Don't call me a bum.

MAX

You know it yourself. You're a bum who never made a living in his life.

SOPHIE

Max. Please! Sit down, Max!

(MAX *reluctantly sits. There is a long pause.*)

MAX

(*Unable to contain himself*)

Bum!

(ALLY *comes out of the bedroom and stands in the corner, listening.*)

SOPHIE

Max! (*She sits* MAX *down again. To* SIDNEY) If you'd get married. If you'd settle down. That's a different thing. Who wants to take your boy away? You think we didn't raise two boys ourselves? You get yourself a decent home for the boy, get back on your feet, nobody would be more happy than us. Am I right, Max?

SIDNEY

You think I wouldn't love that? I'd get married tomorrow if I could find the right woman.

SOPHIE

You mean that, Sidney?

SIDNEY

Of course I mean it.

SOPHIE

Max, if he got married again would you help him out? Would you get him started in a little store some place?

MAX

He won't get married.

SOPHIE

If.

MAX

(*As though the very idea is ludicrous*)

If.

SOPHIE

If!

MAX

(*Thinks it over*)

If? . . . Maybe.

SOPHIE

Then you would.

MAX

I'd help him out. If.

SOPHIE

Would you speak to the rest of the family?

MAX

But a living, that's all. No big deals in Florida. You got to understand that, Sidney. You know your trouble? You never been satisfied just getting along like everybody else. You want to be a millionaire. (MAX, *wound up again, is vehemently wagging his finger at* SIDNEY. SOPHIE *propels him, as if she were pushing a baby carriage, to the other side of the room, as* MAX, *oblivious to the movement, keeps ranting at* SIDNEY) But it don't happen like that. It takes a long time to be a millionaire and a lot of hard work, and that's two things you can't stand. So you get that out of your head. You're not going to make a million dollars overnight, Sidney. Not this year and not ever.

SOPHIE

Do you know anybody, Sidney? Max, can you think of anybody he could marry?

MAX

If you find a nice little woman, and settle down with a nice little store in a nice little town . . .

SIDNEY

Listen. I should drop dead on this spot. That's all I keep thinking about, every minute, every day. But meanwhile, until I can find somebody . . . Listen, we get along beautiful here. If I can just get enough money to cover this payment on the rent. Listen, Max. That'll tide me over till the season, then, if I get some decent weather down here—Easy Street. I mean, I been down a million times but I always bounce back up. And meanwhile I'm all the time looking for women—I mean the right woman.

MAX

Come, Sophie. You talk to him it's like talking, I don't know, to the floor. I tell him a nice little town, a good living, he tells me right away (what does he call it?) Easy Street. You know who lives on Easy Street? I'll tell you. Nobody. Easy Street. I worked hard my whole life. Twelve hours a day, and I made a good living.

SOPHIE

All right, Max.

SIDNEY

What're you getting so excited? Come on. Listen. We'll talk in the morning.

MAX

I never seen a man could make me so mad.

SOPHIE

You'll get all excited you won't be able to sleep.

MAX

All right. We'll go to bed. You got a room? I'll pay you.

SIDNEY

He'll pay me.

MAX

If I sleep in a room . . .

SIDNEY

Don't insult me, will you? I got a beautiful room for you. (*To* ALLY) Get me the key, Ally.

(ALLY *goes to the desk to get the key. By this time, the*

man on the sun deck has moved his chair next to TINA'S *and is sitting with his arm around her.*)

MAX

I'll call up first thing in the morning. We'll make reservations. All right? They got an airplane leaves in the afternoon? Then when I go out to buy the candy—what do we need, Sophie—about seven boxes? I don't think we'll give one this trip to Albert. Albert. Then you can call up those people. Mrs. Rogers. I don't even know Mrs. Rogers. What're you going to call up people you don't even know? At least the Feldmans I know. I don't like them, but I know them at least. (SOPHIE, *preoccupied, is not listening*) Sophie?

SOPHIE

Sidney, I want to ask you a plain question. Will you give me a plain answer?

SIDNEY

For you, honey? Listen.

SOPHIE

I'm very serious.

SIDNEY

(*To* MAX)

When she gets that look in her eyes . . .

SOPHIE

Did you mean it before when you said you'd like to find a nice little woman and settle down?

SIDNEY

I should drop dead on this spot.

MAX

Every time he says that I know it's a lie.

SIDNEY

I mean it.

MAX

If he dropped dead all the times he was supposed to drop dead I'd go in the cemetery business.

(ALLY *comes in with the key.*)

SOPHIE

You know who would be perfect, Max? Mrs. Rogers. Her husband died a couple years ago. You remember, Max. And he left her quite a few dollars, too, and she doesn't have any children, and . . . Sidney, you can believe me. She's a nice quiet little woman and she would be just perfect for you.

MAX

Say, you know what? What's the matter with Louie Bender's second cousin?

SOPHIE

Why do you always say that?

MAX

She's a nice, quiet woman.

SOPHIE

She's old enough to be his mother.

MAX

She's a nice, quiet woman.

SOPHIE

Every time I mention a woman you bring up Louie Bender's second cousin. Is that the only woman you know?

MAX

She's a nice, quiet woman.

SOPHIE

I'm telling you Mrs. Rogers. Remember we used to go to their house? You could eat a meal off the floor—

SIDNEY

If you don't mind—I don't like to eat off the floor!

MAX

(*To* SOPHIE)

All right. If you want Mrs. Rogers . . .

SIDNEY

What're you crazy? You picking out a wife for me like a slave market some place—Arabia?

SOPHIE

She's living right here in Miami now. I'm supposed to call her up and say hello.

SIDNEY

Please, Sophie.

SOPHIE

What's it going to cost you to meet the woman?

MAX

He won't get married.

SOPHIE

You'll take her out a few times. It won't kill you.

MAX

He wants a young girl. A tramp.

SOPHIE

All I ask you, Sidney, think about it. If you want to meet the woman I'll call her up and we'll all get together. There's no harm in that. Will you, Sidney? Will you think about it?

SIDNEY

All right. I'll think about it. Come on. I'll show you the room.

SOPHIE

(*She cries as she kisses* SIDNEY)

I want you to be happy, Sidney. I swear to God.

(SIDNEY *goes to the lobby, gets their luggage, and goes up the stairs.*)

MAX

What're you crying about?

SOPHIE

Good night, Ally.

MAX

She cries.

SOPHIE

(*To* ALLY *tearfully*)

I want you to know . . . both of us . . . we would like it very much . . . for you to live with us. You'd be like my . . . We'd give you everything.

(*She goes up the stairs and exits.*)

MAX

(*To* ALLY)

That Sophie. Everything she cries. You're a good boy, Ally.

(*He pinches* ALLY *on the arm and then joins* SOPHIE. ALLY *is alone in the room. The experience has been almost shattering for him. He goes out to the porch, sits and cries softly.* SIDNEY *comes down the stairs to his room. He turns on the radio, then looks for* ALLY. *Not finding him in the bedroom,* SIDNEY *goes out to the lobby. He sees* ALLY *on the porch and goes to him.*)

SIDNEY

What're you doing out here? (ALLY *won't look at him, just shakes his head.* SIDNEY *gets out his handkerchief, hands it to* ALLY) Go ahead, blow, it's my new handkerchief. (ALLY *takes the handkerchief, starts to use it, and notices the lipstick. He hands it back to* SIDNEY) Listen, Ally. I want to tell you something. I'm a young man. It's not bad if I go out with a girl. Ally, I want you to look at me.

ALLY

You want me to go with them?

SIDNEY

Will you stop it?

ALLY

Tell me the truth.

SIDNEY

The truth? No. I want you to stay with me. But I'll tell you one thing. They're right. You're a very skinny kid. You really are. I told you eat. No. Fried salami. What kind of food is that for a kid to eat?

ALLY

I'm not a kid. I wish you'd stop calling me a kid.

SIDNEY

No. You're an old man with a beard.

ALLY

I'm not a kid.

SIDNEY

You know what let's do? First thing in the morning let's go right out and buy the biggest icebox they ever seen in their life.

One of them fancy kind I seen on television comes in two colors. You know the kind? You push a button, ice cubes fall in your hand.

ALLY

Boy.

SIDNEY

I mean it. And we'll keep milk in there and everything. I'll show them who knows how to take care of a kid.

ALLY

You really get me.

SIDNEY

And vegetables. Everything. All right? You don't like them lousy restaurants? Fine. From now on we're going to eat three meals a day right here in this house.

ALLY

Who's going to cook?

SIDNEY

What's the matter with me? Don't you think I can do anything?

ALLY

I don't think you can cook.

SIDNEY

What's the big deal? I'll get a hot plate. They got all these frozen foods now. Just take the package, dump it in the water.

That's the whole deal. Believe me. Any dumb slob's a cook these days. You like vegetables? Name me a vegetable. We'll get all the vegetables they make.

ALLY

Spinach?

SIDNEY

Spinach. What do I need you for spinach? Spinach, I know. Name me them crazy kind. Broccoli. That kind. We'll get them all.

ALLY

Cauliflower?

SIDNEY

That's no vegetable!

ALLY

What do you think it is?

SIDNEY

Poison!

ALLY

How come we got to eat vegetables?

SIDNEY

So you can grow up, stupid, and nobody's going to go around saying how skinny you are. You think I like that? It makes me look terrible.

ALLY

Boy.

SIDNEY

Boy. What're you boying about? Are you skinny or not?

ALLY

Vegetables *make* you skinny. That's what everybody eats on a diet. When you're trying to get skinny.

SIDNEY

(*Suddenly furious*)

What do you talk back to me so much for? You give me a pain in the neck and I'm sick of it!

(*There is a long pause.* ALLY *is frightened at the fury of* SIDNEY'S *attack.*)

ALLY

Pop? (SIDNEY *comes to* ALLY, *sits down, almost in tears*) I was just kidding.

(*There is a long pause.* ALLY *tries in some way, any way, to comfort him.*)

SIDNEY

What happened, Ally? Everything was so nice. We were just getting on our feet. So what happened? She was so good, Mama. In her whole life she never hurt a fly. Does it make sense? You take a louse, he walks the street, everything. Fine. A man is mean he lives to be a hundred, but your mama was a queen. Does it figure a woman like that has got to die so young? The way she used to look at you. Everybody said it. She used to love you like you were the whole world. I miss her, Ally. She always knew what to do, that woman. In her own quiet little way. She never said a word, but when she opened her mouth she knew what she was talking about. I used to wake up sometimes two, three in the morning and I'd say to her, let's go for a ride. You want a cup of coffee? And she wouldn't get mad. She'd tell me if I wanted to go, she'd go. That's all. And I would just look at her, laying there like a little girl, her sleepy eyes half closed, and I'd realize what a crazy idea it was and we'd both laugh and I'd go back to sleep.

(*There is a long silence as both remember her.*)

ALLY

(*Touching* SIDNEY, *trying so hard to help*)

Pop?

SIDNEY

Pop. He calls me Pop.

ALLY

What do you want me to call you? Father?

SIDNEY

Like a night watchman some place. Pop.

ALLY

I'm not exactly crazy about the way you call me a kid all the time.

SIDNEY

You had some luck, boy. Believe me.

ALLY

A kid is a goat.

SIDNEY

(*Embracing* ALLY)

You know what? You must of been standing behind a pole or something the day they gave out the daddies.

ALLY

We don't have to worry about this place. Do we? I can get a job some place.

(*Pause.*)

SIDNEY

You know what, Ally? I think I'll tell your Aunt Sophie I'd like to meet that woman.

ALLY

What woman?

SIDNEY

The one they want to fix me up with.

ALLY

You want to get married again?

SIDNEY

Who said I've got to marry the woman? I'm just going to meet her. If she turns out to be a dog, fino. At least I met her and then your Uncle Max can't keep calling me a bum all the time.

ALLY

But suppose she turns out to be nice?

SIDNEY

Wonderful! I'll tell you what. I'll ask Sophie first thing in the morning to bring over that broad so we can have a look at her. Okay? If you like her and I like her she's got herself a deal. All right? (ALLY *nods*) Good. It's all settled.

(SIDNEY *gets up and starts for the lobby.*)

ALLY

(*Stopping* SIDNEY)

Pop?

SIDNEY

What?

ALLY

Suppose she don't like us?

SIDNEY

Are you kidding?

(ALLY *starts to laugh, and then* SIDNEY *starts to laugh, too. For a while they are both laughing.* SIDNEY *comes to* ALLY *and gradually they begin scuffling, like two little boys.* SIDNEY *finally holds* ALLY *down, and tickles him.*)

ALLY

I give up. I give up. (SIDNEY *lets him get up and throws him over his shoulder. Then* SHIRL *comes to the window. They both see her. She takes a last breath of fresh night air, and goes back to bed. There is a long pause. Both* SIDNEY *and* ALLY *stop laughing when they see her. They are both very sober now. With* ALLY *still on his shoulder,* SIDNEY *goes toward their bedroom, as* ALLY *speaks again*) Pop?

SIDNEY

What?

ALLY

How about asparagus, eggplant, artichoke, Brussels sprouts, rudibaker, zucchini, squash, turnips . . .

The Curtain Falls

PART TWO

PART TWO

Scene I

Late afternoon. The next day.

In the lobby FRANK *is sitting on the sofa, reading a paper. The radio is playing in* SIDNEY'S *room.*

SIDNEY *enters from his bedroom. He dries his face with a towel, then, alternately putting each foot up on the sofa, he shines his shoes with the towel.* SHIRL *is sitting in her room, combing her hair.* MR. GOLDBLATT *is sunning himself on the sun deck.*

SIDNEY

(*Singing*)

"Love is a many splendored thing . . ."

(*At which point the radio blurts out a commercial about taking a plane to Cuba: "Fly now—pay later."* SIDNEY *listens, agrees, finishes shining his shoes, throws the towel in a corner and goes into his bedroom.* SHIRL *comes down the stairs and into the lobby.*)

SHIRL

Hi, Frank. Mail in yet?

FRANK

Not a thing.

SHIRL

For a change. (ALLY *has come around the corner and now enters the lobby. He is all dressed up, his hair plastered flat against his head, and in his hand a bunch of flowers. To* ALLY) Hi.

ALLY

Hi.

SHIRL

Where you going all dressed up?

ALLY

(*Embarrassed*)

I don't know.

(SHIRL *laughs, goes out to the porch and sits down.*)

FRANK

(*To* ALLY)

What've you got on your head?

ALLY

Why? Don't you like it?

FRANK

You're not supposed to put the whole bottle on. What's going on here today, anyway? Everybody's running around all dressed up. Your aunt's been down here forty times, I bet. Just comes down, looks around and goes back up.

ALLY

We're kind of . . . I don't know . . . expecting company. (*Then* ALLY, *seeing that* SHIRL *is within earshot, gets an idea. He speaks to* FRANK, *but it is really for* SHIRL'S *benefit*) Frank? Can you keep a secret?

FRANK

Well I can I guess, but I don't like to. Why?

ALLY

Never mind. I guess I'd better not.

(*He starts toward his room.*)

FRANK

Wait a minute. Where you going?

ALLY

Promise not to tell anybody?

FRANK

What's going on here?

ALLY

Well . . . how can I put it? . . . We're expecting some company . . . that is, my dad is . . . and . . . I don't know how to say it exactly, but anybody that wants to be a nice guy would go to the beach or something and not be here because . . . I don't know . . . he might be getting married.

FRANK

I don't believe it. Your dad getting married? I didn't even know he was keeping company. (*He notices* SHIRL, *who has come to the door now to see what* ALLY *is trying to do*) I mean for keeps.

ALLY

Okay, Frank?

(*He starts toward his room.*)

FRANK

Wait a minute. What do you mean, go to the beach? I don't . . .

(*He stops, looks over at* SHIRL, *who is glaring at* ALLY. FRANK *puts two and two together.*)

ALLY

I think I said too much already. (*He goes to his room, automatically turning off the radio as he comes in*) Pop?

SIDNEY

(*Coming out*)

Where'd you go? I've been waiting here like a . . . Where's my suit?

ALLY

You know what? Why don't you wear your brown suit.

SIDNEY

I don't want to wear my brown suit. I want to wear my new suit.

ALLY

You look very good in brown.

SIDNEY

I want to wear my new suit.

ALLY

Well . . . it's not ready yet.

SIDNEY

What do you mean, not ready? He promised.

ALLY

Honest. You look just great in brown.

SIDNEY

What's the deal here? What're you selling me?

ALLY

I just don't want you to get all excited and mad and everything and be in a mad mood when . . . you know . . . the lady gets here. That's all. Honest.

SIDNEY

What'd you do? Buy flowers?

ALLY

Twenty-nine cents. You like them?

SIDNEY

Listen. Come here a minute. I want to talk to you. Tell me. Who do you think is coming here? Marilyn Monroe? Some woman is coming here. An old woman. She'll come in, we'll say hello. It's a nice day. Good-bye. So what're you making a big production?

ALLY

I don't see where a couple of flowers is a big production.

SIDNEY

Well, you take it easy. That's all. You know what you're doing? Building yourself up for a big letdown. Think I never had a blind date before? You think she's going to be Marilyn Monroe, but let me tell you.

ALLY

I don't see where Marilyn Monroe's so great. You keep talking about Marilyn Monroe. What's so great about Marilyn Monroe?

SIDNEY

Come around in about five years. I'll tell you.

ALLY

Oh. That.

SIDNEY

What?

ALLY

I know.

SIDNEY

What you know?

ALLY

I know.

SIDNEY

Don't know so much. You're a little kid. I'll tell you when to know. (ALLY *moves away from him. His feelings are hurt.* MRS. FESSLER *and* HERBERT *come around the corner and into the lobby, then go through the hall to their room*) Hey, moody? What're you so moody?

ALLY

Can I just ask you one favor?

SIDNEY

I know.

ALLY

What?

SIDNEY

Be nice to her. Right?

ALLY

Just don't be grouchy, that's all, because even if she don't look exactly like Marilyn Monroe she might be okay once you get to know her. You know what I mean?

SIDNEY

(*Goes to* ALLY. *Pause*)

You want this pretty bad, don't you?

ALLY

I wouldn't say that.

SIDNEY

(*Pulling* ALLY *to him*)
You wouldn't, huh? What would you say?

ALLY

Come on.

SIDNEY

Huh?

ALLY

You know.

SIDNEY

Listen. (*He takes* ALLY *in his arms. There is a very tender moment, then* SIDNEY *begins sniffing and when he realizes what it is he smells, he pushes* ALLY *away from him*) What're you, crazy? What've you got on your head?

ALLY

I know. It's terrible.

SIDNEY

Get inside there and wash your head off.

ALLY

It's not that bad.

SIDNEY

Believe me. It's that bad. (*He aims* ALLY *toward the bathroom*) I'll run next door and get my suit.
(*He starts out.*)

ALLY

Pop?

SIDNEY

What?

ALLY

You could always wear your brown suit.

SIDNEY

Hey, nag-o! (*He goes out to the lobby after turning on the radio*) What do you say, Frank? Anything new?

FRANK

Congratulations!

SIDNEY

For what? (FRANK *whistles "Here Comes the Bride"*) Take a walk, will you? (SHIRL *gets up and stands so that she is blocking the doorway to the porch.* SIDNEY *sees this and decides he has to get rid of* FRANK. MRS. FESSLER *and* HERBERT *come onto the sun deck and sit.* SIDNEY *turns to* FRANK) Did you fix that bed yet? In thirty-four?

FRANK

You told me to watch the board.

SIDNEY

Don't tell me what I told you. I'm telling you thirty four.

(FRANK *goes up the stairs and exits.* SIDNEY *goes to* SHIRL. *For a long moment they just glare at each other.*)

SHIRL

(*Finally, with a catlike gesture*)

Psssttt.

SIDNEY

What's that for?

SHIRL

I'm checking out.

SIDNEY

Don't kid around. (*She continues to look at him, and is very serious. She shakes her head*) What're you trying to do? Make everything, my whole blood, drain out of me?

(*She looks at him again and sees that he really means it. Then she changes her tone, instantly and completely.*)

SHIRL

Want to see a monkey?

(*She holds the mirror up to him.*)

SIDNEY

Come on. I'll buy you a drink.

SHIRL

Hello.

(*She kisses him.*)

SIDNEY

Hey, kook. You know you're a kook? Like a cuckoo. A kook. One minute you knife me, then you kiss me. What do you, love me or hate me?

SHIRL

I'm a kook. You like kooks?

SIDNEY

That's my weakness.

SHIRL

Who's the woman?

SIDNEY

What woman?

SHIRL

You're seeing a woman.

SIDNEY

No kidding. Is that what you're mad at? Is that the whole thing? I thought I really done something.

SHIRL

Keep going.

SIDNEY

Listen, Shirl. I've got to get some money. Okay? So my brother wants me to meet this woman. So I'll meet her. I'll tell her what he wants to hear, I got it made.

SHIRL

What does he want to hear?

SIDNEY

What?

SHIRL

Does he want you to settle down, get married, make a nice home for the kid?

SIDNEY

What's the difference?

SHIRL

Why don't you?

SIDNEY

What?

SHIRL

You better make up your mind, landlord. What kind of life do you want? You want to be like everybody else, with a home and a kid and the green grass growing all around? Good. That's very easy. You want to be like me? A bird with no tomorrow? That's easy, too. But you can't be them both.

SIDNEY

Come on. I'll buy you a drink.

SHIRL

I'm not thirsty.

SIDNEY

I can't talk here. I'm expecting my brother any minute.

SHIRL

Buy *him* a drink.

SIDNEY

What do you love to needle me? Is that your hobby?

SHIRL

What am I supposed to do? Turn into a pumpkin every time you mention his name? What do I care about your brother? I don't even care about my *own* brother.

SIDNEY

Who said anything?

SHIRL

You know what? It's getting very complicated. Life among the coconuts. I've got that old feeling the wall's are closing in.

SIDNEY

Listen, will you?

SHIRL

All I did was say hello. You said hello. We smiled and hit the sack. A perfect friendship. But now, all of a sudden . . . It's bad enough we've got to sneak around your kid don't catch us, but now I can't even stand in the lobby. And you know the worst part of it? I'm beginning to care about it, and that's what bothers me.

SIDNEY

You do want me, don't you?

SHIRL

But I don't want to settle down with a twelve-year-old kid. Not yet, at least. I just got started. Why do you think I finally left my husband? Him and the whole Coxie's Army, his family, kept nudging me, day after day, have a baby. Have a baby. Who's got the time to have a baby? All I want is to do what I want, when I want, how I want and where. So you better make up your mind, landlord. You going to be a solid citizen or a bird like me?

SIDNEY

We'll talk about it later. Okay? I'll meet you for dinner. We'll take a ride. We'll figure it out.

SHIRL

I thought you're going to meet some woman.

SIDNEY

How long can that take? Fifteen, twenty minutes. And then we'll take off. Me and you. Okay, Shirl? What do you say?

SHIRL

I don't know. If I had one brain in working condition . . .

SIDNEY

You know what I want?

SHIRL

Sure. Everything. Like a little kid. Gimme. Gimme. Gimme.

SIDNEY

Listen, Shirl. I'll meet you . . . say in a half an hour. Okay? We'll go out have a nice dinner. You know the Copa? The owner's a personal friend of mine, and then . . . what a beautiful idea! . . . We'll drive out the airport and hop a plane for Cuba. Huh? It's only fifty-nine minutes away. "Fly now—brrrp—pay later!"? We'll get there, dance a couple cha-cha-chas, have a nice Cuban breakfast and I'll have you back here in time for the morning papers. (*She starts to laugh*) What? What're you laughing?

SHIRL

A couple of cha-cha-chas?

SIDNEY

What's the matter? I'm a good dancer. Get me on that floor, I'm light as a feather.

SHIRL

I'll get you on that floor.

SIDNEY

Shirl, honey . . . what do you say? A date?

SHIRL

(*There is a long pause as she looks at him*)

You got a quarter?

(MAX *appears on the sun deck and starts down the stairs.*)

SIDNEY

What?

SHIRL

Let me borrow it a minute.

SIDNEY

(*Gives it to her*)

What're you doing? (*She flips the coin, looks at it, then hands it back to him*) Okay?

SHIRL

Okay.

(SIDNEY *and* SHIRL *start to dance.* MAX *comes into the lobby.* SIDNEY *sees him and quickly pretends to be doing something else, pushing* SHIRL *aside.*)

SIDNEY

Max! How are you?

(SHIRL *just stands there to tantalize* SIDNEY.)

MAX

That's a Sidney? Some Sidney!

SIDNEY

What'd you, buy a new tie? That's very nice.

MAX

What new? I had it two, three years already. I bought it special Louie Bender's son got married. A fine boy. Made a lot of money. (SIDNEY *is trying to keep* MAX *from seeing him as he motions for* SHIRL *to get out of there*) You dressed?

SIDNEY

What?

MAX

Like that you're going to meet a woman?

SIDNEY

What're you, crazy? I'm getting my new suit. Come on, walk me over.

MAX

My feet hurt.

SIDNEY

That's the best thing. Walking. Good for the circulation.

SHIRL

Walking? (*To* MAX) Where do they hurt you?

MAX

Right here. On the bottom.

SHIRL

Here? That's very bad. The metatarsal.

MAX

(*Impressed*)

Yeah?

SHIRL

Ever try hot water? That's very good for it.

MAX

Yeah? I don't know. I tried a couple times Epsom salts. You

know Epsom salts? I put it on but nothing happened. My feet got salty. (*To* SIDNEY) What're you standing? The woman'll be here any minute.

SIDNEY

Come on—you thirsty? I'll buy you a drink.

MAX

Big shot. He'll buy me a drink. (*To* SHIRL) You live here?

SHIRL

Come on, Sidney. Introductions are in order. Never mind—I'll do it. (*Introducing them*) Max, meet Sidney. Sidney, this is your brother Max. My name is Mud—Miss Mud!

(*She goes up the stairs to her room.*)

MAX

Who's that? (SIDNEY *shrugs*) She looks like a chorus girl, but she talks like a foot doctor.

(SOPHIE *comes down the stairs from the sun deck.*)

SIDNEY

Look! (*He sings*) "A pretty girl is like a mel-o-dy!" Max, I'll make you a deal. I'll take Sophie and give you Mrs. Roberts and six points.

(*He kisses* SOPHIE *and goes out.*)

SOPHIE

(*Calling after him*)

Rogers! Sidney, where are you going? Where is he going, Max?

MAX

To get his suit.

SOPHIE

Now? She'll be here any minute. So how come she didn't come already? Look what time it is?

MAX

What're you so nervous? You told her five o'clock. That's what it is. Look. One minute she's late.

SOPHIE

Your watch.

MAX

All right. Five minutes. Ten minutes. She'll be here. How wrong can a watch be?

SOPHIE

You like this dress better?

MAX

To me you looked very good before.

SOPHIE

Maybe she came already and didn't find us so she went away.

MAX

She didn't go away so quick. I guarantee you.

(MRS. ROGERS *comes around the corner and up to the porch.* MAX *and* SOPHIE, *in the lobby, do not see her.*)

SOPHIE

Uh huh. He's starting already.

MAX

What'd I say?

SOPHIE

She's a very sensitive woman and, I'm telling you, if you say one thing to hurt her feelings . . .

MAX

What? What? What're you talking?

SOPHIE

I know you. Just keep quiet and don't say anything, we'll be all right.

MAX

What's she, doing me a favor? I'll tell her in a minute. Don't do me no favors.

SOPHIE

(*Sees* MRS. ROGERS)

Max! (*She goes to meet* MRS. ROGERS) Hello! How are you? Max, look who's here. Let me look at you. You lost a little weight.

MRS. ROGERS

No. I'm about the same.

SOPHIE

You remember my husband Max.

MRS. ROGERS

Of course. How are you?

SOPHIE

Don't you think she lost a little weight, Max?

MAX

The woman just told you she didn't lose, what're you making her out a skeleton?

SOPHIE

My husband. Whatever I say he's got an answer. Come inside. I'm so anxious for you to meet Sidney. We've told him so much about you. He just went out for a minute. He'll be right back. (*They go into* SIDNEY's *room.* MAX *closes the door*) You like this place? He's fixed it up very nice. You should have seen it before he took over. What a difference. Like night and day.

(SOPHIE *motions for* MAX *to get* ALLY.)

MAX

(*Knocks on the bedroom door*)

Ally?

(*He opens the door without waiting for anybody to answer.* ALLY *comes out and goes right over and turns off the radio.*)

SOPHIE

Ally, come here, honey. I want you to meet Mrs. Rogers. This is my nephew Ally.

MAX

(*Confidentially*)

That's the son.

(*There is a long pause.* MRS. ROGERS *and* ALLY *look at each other. Love at first sight.*)

MRS. ROGERS

How do you do.

ALLY

How do you do.

SOPHIE

Sit down. What're we standing? Here. Sit down here, Mrs. Rogers. (*Indicating the modern chair*) Make yourself comfortable.

MAX

(*To* MRS. ROGERS)

Don't take that chair. You'll never get up!

SOPHIE

Here's a nice chair.

MAX

You like this chair?

MRS. ROGERS

(*Sitting on sofa*)

Fine. That's fine. Thanks.

SOPHIE

I'll take the crazy chair.

MAX

Don't be such a hero. You want to break your back? (*To* MRS. ROGERS) She's got a terrible back as it is. No. She wants another doctor bill.

SOPHIE

One of our boys, Robert, is a doctor. Did you know that?

MRS. ROGERS

No. I didn't.

SOPHIE

He just finished up last year and Max opened him up a beautiful office on Park Avenue in New York.

MAX

I told him. We got so much sickness in the family he could make a living on that alone.

SOPHIE

Our other boy, Albert, is in the store with us. He's married.

MAX

Albert.

SOPHIE

Max!

MAX

He's in the store? He sits there. A customer comes in—he runs in the toilet. (SOPHIE *is glaring at* MAX. SIDNEY *comes into the lobby. As he hears their voices, he hesitates and goes behind the desk*) What're you looking? A big secret. She'll be in the family—she'll know anyway. (*There is an awkward pause.*)

SOPHIE

(*Trying to save the situation*)

Well, it certainly has been a long time.

MRS. ROGERS

That's right. It has been.

SOPHIE

Remember, Max? She came over to the house one Sunday.

MAX

I don't exactly remember, to be honest.

SOPHIE

Sure you do. One Sunday. We had the store in North Carolina.

MAX

She tells me I do. I don't remember.

SOPHIE

Max! Now stop it.

MAX

What do you want me to do? Lie? All right. I remember.

(SIDNEY *is standing at the desk, trying to decide what to do.*)

ALLY

Can I get somebody a Pepsi-Cola or something?

MAX

Good. I was just going to ask you. (*He pinches* ALLY'S *arm*) I got such a bad taste in my mouth. Must be that pastrami this morning. (*To* MRS. ROGERS) I had pastrami and eggs.

SOPHIE

You don't need any soda, Max.

MAX

You ever seen a woman in your life? She's in love with plain water. All right. I'll have water. You got some water?

ALLY

Sure. Anybody else?

SOPHIE

All right. I'll have some water.

ALLY

(*To* MRS. ROGERS)

Can I get you something?

MRS. ROGERS

Not right now. Thank you very much.

ALLY

It's no trouble. Really.

MRS. ROGERS

All right. I'll have some water too.

(ALLY *goes into the bedroom.*)

SOPHIE

He's such a nice little boy.

MAX

Ally? Wonderful boy.

SOPHIE

And he's very smart in school, too.

MAX

Quiet? He never says a word.

SIDNEY

(*Calling* FRANK *in the back office*)

Frank?

SOPHIE

He reminds me a lot of my son Robert.

MAX

Yeah. That's right. He looks like Robert.

SOPHIE

They don't look at all alike, but they have the same ways.

MAX

I'm telling you. Him and Robert. One face. I'll show you the picture.

(*He reaches for his wallet.*)

SOPHIE

Leave her alone with your pictures. You know the Museum in New York of Pictures? That's Max in his pocket.

SIDNEY

(*As* FRANK *comes out*)

Listen, Frank. I want you to do me a favor. In about ten minutes you call me in there. All right? Tell me there's some kind of emergency. I don't care what, but tell me it's very important and I've got to be there right away. All right?

FRANK

Leave it to me.

(SIDNEY *starts toward his room.*)

MAX

Here. He's nine years old, my Robert. Where'd we take this picture, Sophie? In Rockaway?

SIDNEY

(*Returning to* FRANK)

On second thought you just call me. I'll make up my own emergency. I know you.

MAX

Look at that face. I'm telling you. Him and Ally. One face.

SOPHIE

In the first place, Ally's skin and bones, and Robert, thank God, even if he is my son . . .

SIDNEY

(*Bursting into the room*)

Hi, Max! Sophie! This is Mrs. Roberts?

SOPHIE

Mrs. Ro*gers!*

SIDNEY

I'm awful sorry I'm late. Pleased to meet you, Mrs. Rogers. Where's Ally?

SOPHIE

In the other room.

MAX

You want to see the pictures?

SOPHIE

Max, put away the pictures.

SIDNEY

What's Max, showing you his pictures? I've seen them all already a hundred times.

MAX

I've got some new ones.

SOPHIE

Max.

(*She motions for him to put them away. He does so reluctantly.*)

SIDNEY

That Max and his pictures. (ALLY *comes out with the water*) There he is. You meet my son Alvin?

ALLY

Alvin?

SIDNEY

All right. He hates that name. (*To* ALLY) What're you doing? Water? Why don't you get some soda?

ALLY

They don't want soda.

SIDNEY

Is that what you wanted? Water? Okay. Get me a water. (ALLY *goes out*) That's the best thing for you. Water. It cleans out your blood. How are you, Max? You get on the beach today?

MAX

Sure. Right away.

SOPHIE

In twenty years he never went in the water. Not once.

MAX

That's no fun by me. You sit there. You get hot. You go in the water you get cold. You come out. You get hot again. You call this pleasure?

SIDNEY

You used to love the Turkish baths? Remember?

MAX

That's different. You go to the baths, you take off your clothes, you meet people!

SIDNEY

We used to go there as kids. Remember? Fifty cents you could sleep the whole night.

MAX

Now it costs you ten, twelve dollars.

SIDNEY

I'll tell you what. Next time I come to New York we'll go. All right? Me and you. I didn't go, I bet, twenty years. What do you say, Max? A date?

MAX

I don't make dates. You come, we'll talk about it.

SIDNEY

That Max. He wouldn't commit himself no matter what. I could fix him up with Marilyn Monroe, y'know what he'd say? "We'll talk about it."

SOPHIE

Sidney, you shouldn't make me laugh so much. My back!

MAX

He's such a funny fellow. He don't have an enemy in the world. Huh, Sidney? Am I right?

SOPHIE

That Sidney.

MAX

In the whole family he's the only one makes you laugh.

SIDNEY

You know the black sheep? That's me. Me and my brother Frankie. Say. What's this I hear? I hear Frankie's doing very good now.

MAX

Frankie? He made a lot of money.

SIDNEY

No kidding.

MAX

He bought some property. Everything.

SIDNEY

You see that? There's hope for me, then. Right? If that dope can make it. (*To* MRS. ROGERS) There's eight of us in the family. Eight boys. You want to see a mad house, you ought to see all of us together. We kill each other.

MRS. ROGERS

I think it's wonderful to have such a large family.

SIDNEY

Wonderful? You ought to meet everybody. Max here is the leader. Whatever he says, goes. Right, Max?

MAX

(*Proudly, shyly*)

I'm the oldest.

SIDNEY

Maybe once every ten years we all get together, and even that's too often.

SOPHIE

What're you talking so much? You'll make her think the family's no good.

SIDNEY

I'm just kidding. The lady knows that. (ALLY *comes out with the water. He gives it to* SIDNEY, *who drinks it all down in one swig, like medicine*) That's wonderful. Water. Why don't I drink it more? Soda. You drink a gallon it only makes you more thirsty. You want some more? Ally, get some more water.

MAX

Not for me.

SOPHIE

I didn't finish this yet.

ALLY

(*To* MRS. ROGERS)

Can I get you some more?

MRS. ROGERS

Not right now. Thank you.

(*There is an awkward pause.*)

SIDNEY

(*Suddenly, to* ALLY)

Tell me quick for one million dollars. Who did Tommy Burns win the heavyweight crown from, in how many rounds?

ALLY

Not right now, Pop.

SIDNEY

Come on. Don't be bashful.

ALLY

He won it from Marvin Hart in 1906. Twenty rounds.

SIDNEY

Correct! For one million dollars. That kid knows them all. He could go on that sixty-four-thousand-dollar program tomorrow and win in two minutes. (*To* MRS. ROGERS) You like boxing?

MRS. ROGERS

Well, I don't know very much about it.

SIDNEY

I know. Women don't seem to like it, somehow. Don't ask me why.

MAX

Sidney, you going to talk about fights?

SIDNEY

Listen. It's a dying field of sports. You take when I was a kid, we really had some fighters in my time, but now, they're all a bunch of bums. There's nobody to get the public interest nowadays.

MAX

Sidney, you don't mind, it's getting late. I think we ought to get down to business. All right?

SIDNEY

What're you talking about?

MAX

I got some good news for you. I called the whole family this morning and we had a good talk.

SIDNEY

All right, Max. Good. You'll tell me later.

MAX

Everybody's going to chip in a few dollars, and we all decided. I got this nice little property in Marion, a very nice little town, and I wouldn't lie to you, this store's a one hundred percent location.

SIDNEY

Max?

MAX

(SOPHIE *tugs at* MAX's *jacket in an effort to keep him from saying anything more. He is oblivious, straightens his coat and continues*)

. . . And the people was in it, a chain store, just built a place across the street, so my store is empty. Tell them, Sophie. Is that a beautiful store?

SOPHIE

Max.

MAX

A thirty-foot front. Three windows. Well, anyhow. We all decided. (SOPHIE *again pulls his coat tail*) You'll open up a nice little five-and-ten there you'll be all right. There's only one junky little place in the whole town. For years I been talking about it myself, opening up a five-and-ten there, so I guarantee you. (SOPHIE *tugs his jacket once more. Again* MAX *is unaware of it. He adjusts his coat and continues*) You'll both work in the store, you'll watch the pennies, you'll make a very nice living. (*To* MRS. ROGERS) Believe me. You'll like this town very much. You'll find a nice little house, and you won't have to worry. On our side we'll all chip in, give you five thousand dollars, and I understand your husband left you a few dollars? . . .

MRS. ROGERS

(*Gets up. She is feeling dizzy, nauseated*)

Excuse me.

(*She goes to the porch.*)

SIDNEY

(*To* MAX)

What're you, crazy?

SOPHIE

(*Goes to* MAX, *hitting him lightly on the head*)

Dummy. You dummy. What's the matter with you? Dummy.

MAX

What'd I say?

SOPHIE

Just like that you make a proposition? What's the matter with you?

MAX

She came here, I thought we'll talk.

SOPHIE

Like that?

MAX

What'd I say?

SOPHIE

You apologize. You hear me?

MAX

I thought I'm doing a good thing.

SOPHIE

You can't talk to people that way.

MAX

The woman came here, a grown-up woman. What'd she come here for? I thought we'll talk.

SIDNEY

Listen, Ally. He don't mean anything. He's a dumb jerk.

MAX

I'm dumb?

SIDNEY

Dumb? You're stupid.

MAX

So what do you come to me for, I'm so stupid? You need money I'm not so stupid.

SIDNEY

What do you think? You're in China some place? She's a human being, that woman. You think nobody's got any feelings? All of a sudden you got a package deal. She'll put up so much, you'll put up so much. Fine. You're in business.

MAX

You're a grown-up man. Let me tell you. I met Sophie the same way. (SOPHIE *slams the door closed so that* MRS. ROGERS *won't hear.* MAX *turns to* SOPHIE) You don't remember? All of a sudden she's a big society woman. We'll send out invitations. I came over the house one Sunday, we talked a few minutes and your father made the arrangements. Did it work out so terrible? That was over thirty years ago, and I couldn't ask for a better life. I don't know. I'm a terrible man. Everybody looks at me.

(MRS. ROGERS *comes back into the room. There is a brief pause. She has composed herself.*)

MRS. ROGERS

You want to know how much money I have?

MAX

Believe me . . . They all look at me I did a terrible thing. I didn't mean to hurt your feelings. I'm a plain man. Maybe I said it wrong. I'm sorry. Believe me. If I hurt your feelings, on my mother's grave, I apologize.

SIDNEY

Max, will you get out of here?

MAX

Don't be such a . . .

SIDNEY

(*To* SOPHIE)

Get him out of here.

MAX

. . . big shot.

SOPHIE

Max! Come on. (MAX *goes upstairs.* SOPHIE *speaks to* MRS. ROGERS) I'll call you later. All right? I'm sorry. I apologize for my husband.

MAX

(*Hears* SOPHIE *and comes racing down the stairs*)

Don't apologize. What'd I do? Apologize. I did already. Didn't you hear me apologize?

SOPHIE

Max, get up those stairs! Why do you always do that?

(*They exit, still arguing. There is a long awkward pause.*)

ALLY

(*To* MRS. ROGERS)

Excuse me.

(*He looks at her, and then, spontaneously, she hugs him. He goes to the lobby and into the back office.*)

MRS. ROGERS

He's a very sweet boy.

SIDNEY

Ally? There's nothing like him. (*Another awkward pause*) Listen. About my brother . . .

MRS. ROGERS

That's all right. I'm sorry I let it affect me that way.

SIDNEY

Would you believe that dumb jerk can barely read and write his own name? Go figure. A man like that makes a fortune.

MRS. ROGERS

He's not a bad man. At least he didn't strike me as one.

SIDNEY

Who said bad? He's stupid, that's all.

MRS. ROGERS

I just wasn't prepared for such straightforwardness.

SIDNEY

You know, I really couldn't believe it. I heard him talking but I couldn't believe I was hearing it.

MRS. ROGERS

I've never gone through quite this sort of thing before.

SIDNEY

Who has?

MRS. ROGERS

(*Sitting on sofa*)

I guess we'll laugh about it eventually.

SIDNEY

(*Joining her on sofa*)

You know, I didn't picture you like this. You know?

MRS. ROGERS

Disappointed?

SIDNEY

You kidding? I pictured some little old woman straight off the boat, if my brother Max picked her out . . . (*He laughs*) How'd you picture me?

MRS. ROGERS

Well . . . different.

SIDNEY

Better?

MRS. ROGERS

Just different.

SIDNEY

You think I'd be an old man?

MRS. ROGERS

No. They told me your age.

SIDNEY

What else?

MRS. ROGERS

You're very nice. You have a son.

SIDNEY

I mean how I look.

MRS. ROGERS

She said you're very handsome. Like a doctor.

SIDNEY

Some doctor.

MRS. ROGERS

That's what she said.

SIDNEY

Any man wears a clean shirt every day is a doctor by them.

MRS. ROGERS

What I don't understand, though, is . . . well, you don't look like the kind of man who would have any trouble meeting a woman.

SIDNEY

What'd you expect? A mouse?

MRS. ROGERS

In a way. If you want to call it that.

SIDNEY

So how come you came here? You like a mouse?

MRS. ROGERS

I thought you'd be very timid.

SIDNEY

Is that the kind of man you like?

MRS. ROGERS

Should I be frank?

SIDNEY

Sure.

MRS. ROGERS

What I like has very little to do with my life any more. It's just you reach a point, finally, when something is better than nothing at all.

SIDNEY

You mean it wouldn't make any difference? Say you walk in the door and I'm standing there. Frankenstein. You know? The ugliest man you ever seen. What then?

MRS. ROGERS

That depends on what you mean by ugly.

SIDNEY

Ugly. What does ugly mean? Ugly. "He looks ugly."

MRS. ROGERS

No. It doesn't make too much difference to me, frankly. How a person looks.

SIDNEY

Honest?

MRS. ROGERS

If he's a nice person.

SIDNEY

You think a lot of women are like that?

MRS. ROGERS

Looks aren't too important.

SIDNEY

You know, that's terrible, when you come to think about it. It shouldn't be that way. You take the ugliest men in the world usually wind up with the prettiest women.

MRS. ROGERS

If you're going to spend every day of your life with somebody, there are more important things involved than how a woman . . . how a person looks.

SIDNEY

Sure. But you don't want somebody's going to turn your stomach every time you look at them.

MRS. ROGERS

I don't think anybody's that ugly.

SIDNEY

Are you kidding? I used to know two cousins, Joe with-the-mustache, and Joe without. Well them two guys. They were the world's champion ugly. I'm not joking. When we were kids, it came Halloween, all they had to do was go out with their own bare faces. So what happens? They both make a big score in the wholesale beer business and both of them, I swear to God, winds up with the most beautiful chorus girl you'd ever want to see.

MRS. ROGERS

I'm afraid I don't quite understand the point you're trying to make.

SIDNEY

The point is, if you got a lot of money you can afford to go ahead and be ugly, but if you don't have a dime you're in trouble.

MRS. ROGERS

Well, in any case, you don't have to worry about that problem.

SIDNEY

Listen.

MRS. ROGERS

Do you?

SIDNEY

I don't know.

(*He laughs, embarrassed.*)

MRS. ROGERS

I'm sorry. Does that embarrass you?

SIDNEY

(*Rises, goes to radio and turns it on*)

Sure. But I like it.

MRS. ROGERS

I almost didn't get here today. It's really very funny. I kept walking around the block, and every time I'd get in front of the hotel, I'd say, All right, now. This is silly. This time I'm really going in there. What can possibly happen to me? What am I so afraid of? . . . And then I'd get almost to the door . . . (*She laughs*) It was really very funny.

SIDNEY

I'm glad you finally made it.

MRS. ROGERS

Are you?

SIDNEY

You know what you got? One of them inferior conflicts. (*She smiles at him*) What're you laughing?

MRS. ROGERS

Is that my trouble?

SIDNEY

Did I say it wrong?

MRS. ROGERS

Where'd you learn about that?

SIDNEY

From my kid, Ally. He reads more books than any person I ever seen, all kinds of things, you won't believe this, but he reads two, three books a week. This thick. I told him he's going to ruin his eyes but he won't listen to me.

MRS. ROGERS

You know, you're very lucky.

SIDNEY

Me? That's my whole trouble.

MRS. ROGERS

You've got a son.

SIDNEY

Sure, but you don't know. A guy like me. What do I know about kids?

MRS. ROGERS

You know the worst part of my day—having to walk into the grocery store and order one lamb chop, or a pint of milk. A pint of milk. Should I tell you something else?

SIDNEY

Sure.

MRS. ROGERS

That's why I came here. I can't do it any more. No matter what. You'd think after six years of living alone I'd be used to it, but I still can't believe it. I wake up in the morning and there's one second before I'm fully awake when I'm sure everything is different. I know my husband is there . . . and then I open my eyes and I'm forced to realize where I am and who I am and what I've got, and I know that . . . when a person . . . Last week I went for two whole days without saying a word, not even good morning, to a single human being.

SIDNEY

I know. It takes a long time.

MRS. ROGERS

I know.

(SHIRL *comes into her room from her dressing room.*)

SIDNEY

My wife. You know she was only four feet eleven? Honest. We used to look so crazy, her and me. And that big difference in our size? That's only half the difference in our characters. Me. I'm a dope. I never read a book in my life. When I write my name it looks like a kid eight years old. (ALLY *comes out from the inner office and sits reading in the lobby*) No. Really. I couldn't write a letter to sombody if you killed me. But she was really what you call smart, and she didn't go much farther in school than I did. I quit in six B. She went to seven A. But she could spell words I never even heard of. Really. Constantinople. That was nothing for her. I'll tell you the truth. May she rest in peace. She was the sweetest woman in this whole world, but . . . I used to play around once in a while. Isn't that terrible? That's me. I don't have any will power. That's my whole trouble. And I get restless, too. We used to have a store. One store? We went bankrupt the first of every month like clockwork. I hated to stay in the store. You sit around, wait all day for some farmer to come in, buy a nickel spool of thread. You know what I mean? You're stuck there. Okay. So you work twelve hours a day. What's the most you can hope for? A little house some place, a car maybe. You make a nice living. Have a couple of kids. Nothing.

(FRANK *comes out of the inner office and sits at the lobby desk.*)

MRS. ROGERS

Nothing? What else is there?

SIDNEY

You know? It's a funny thing. Just now when I was saying it, for the first time in my life it didn't sound ridiculous, somehow.

MRS. ROGERS

To me, having a home and children . . . (*She laughs*) It's so peculiar. To you I suppose a million dollars is your idea of success and you probably feel a hundred years away from it. Well, that's how far away from my ideal . . . (*She stops, self-consciously*) I didn't mean to imply you'll never get what you want, because to me you definitely seem like the kind of man who will always get exactly what he wants.

SIDNEY

You know what's nice talking to you? You answer me back in all the right places. (*She laughs*) I'm really glad to meet you, or did I say that already?

MRS. ROGERS

I'm glad too. I was so afraid you'd think I was just some

frustrated Miss Lonesome, strictly out to catch a man by hook or by . . . (*She stops. There is a long pause. This is something extremely difficult for her to say, but she has to say it*) No. I can't say that. I'm sorry, but I don't have any right to. I came here . . . I did . . . because I want a husband.

SIDNEY

You're very nice, Mrs. Rogers. I really mean that. I can't understand why any man wouldn't snap you up in a minute.

MRS. ROGERS

Louise.

SIDNEY

Louise. (*They are very close together now, emotionally. Pause. Then* FRANK *rings the phone in the room.* SIDNEY *goes to the phone*) All right, Frank.

FRANK

It's snowing out here in the lobby.

SIDNEY

All right! Will you? (*He hangs up*) That Frank.

MRS. ROGERS

(*Getting up*)

Well. It's been very good to meet you.

SIDNEY

Sit down. Where you running?

MRS. ROGERS

It's all right. I understand. My husband used to have our clerk call us every time he wanted to go home early from a party.

SIDNEY

Listen. I'll tell you the truth. Okay? You're right. I told him to call me.

MRS. ROGERS

Really. You don't have to . . .

SIDNEY

I'll tell you the truth! I got roped into this. My brother was giving me the needles he's going to take away my kid. You know? I asked him lend me some money, he thinks I'm a bum. And my kid, too. He was beginning to look at me funny, so I figured, Okay, they want me to meet a woman, what's it going to cost me? You know? At least they'll say, Okay, I tried.

MRS. ROGERS

It's very nice of you to be so honest with me. Really.

SIDNEY

But I didn't expect you to be like this. You know what I mean?

MRS. ROGERS

I appreciate it. I really do.

(*She gets ready to go, and actually reaches the door before he stops her.*)

SIDNEY

Would you go out with me tonight?

MRS. ROGERS

You don't have to.

SIDNEY

I want to.

MRS. ROGERS

Don't play games with me.

(*She goes to the porch.*)

SIDNEY

(*Following her*)

Listen. You ever been to the Copa? The owner is a personal friend of mine. (*She looks at him, shakes her head*) I want you to. I mean it. We'll have a good dinner. Everything.

MRS. ROGERS

(*Shaking her head*)

Thank you very much.

SIDNEY

What're you, crazy? (*Not wishing to talk in front of* ALLY, *She goes back into* SIDNEY's *room*) I'm asking you to go out with me. I like you. Look in my face. (*She does*) No. Come over here and look. Can't you tell in my face? I like you very much, Louise. So, what do you say? We got a date?

MRS. ROGERS

You come to my place. I'll cook dinner for you.

SIDNEY

You don't have to do that.

MRS. ROGERS

I want to.

SIDNEY

What're you going to stand in a hot kitchen?

MRS. ROGERS

Let me tell you something—for two whole years I went out on dates. I'm tired of dates. I'm tired of talking about nothing and forcing myself to smile trying to make an impression. So, please. Don't ask me to go to a night club. If you take me there I won't know what to say. If you ask me to dance I'll step on your feet. I'll sit there stiff and smiling the whole night and at the end you won't know a thing about me. But I want you to know me. And I want to know you and I want a home, a child. So if you don't want that, what I want, please, tell me now and I'll walk out of here, no feelings hurt—I promise you.

SIDNEY

(*After a moment*)

You know how to make chopped liver?

MRS. ROGERS

With chicken fat, and turnips on the side?

SIDNEY

That's what I love.

MRS. ROGERS

Wonderful! Chopped liver first, and then sweet and sour cabbage—and potato pancakes?

SIDNEY

Honey, you got yourself a deal. You sit here a minute. Okay? Two minutes I'm dressed. (*He goes to the closet and takes out two suits*) You like this suit? What should I wear? You like this blue one?

MRS. ROGERS

The brown one is nice.

SIDNEY

Good. I'll wear the brown one. Two minutes. Okay?

MRS. ROGERS

I'll wait outside in the lobby.

(SIDNEY *goes to the bedroom.* MRS. ROGERS *stands for a moment, looking after him. Then she drinks the last of the water in her glass and goes to the lobby. She sees* ALLY *sitting there with his book, and joins him.*)

ALLY

You're not leaving, are you?

(SHIRL *stands up in her bedroom, combs her hair and gets ready to leave.*)

MRS. ROGERS

I'm just waiting for your father to change his clothes. And then we're going out together.

ALLY

(*After an awkward moment*)

Do you know much about dinosaurs?

MRS. ROGERS

(*Sits down next to* ALLY)

Not too much. A little . . .

FRANK

(*Going up stairs*)

Will you watch the board a minute? Must be a leak on the second floor. It's dripping through in the office.

ALLY

Sure.

MRS. ROGERS

(*To* ALLY)

What about you? Will you be all right? How will you get dinner?

ALLY

I'm going to eat with my Uncle Max. They already invited me.

MRS. ROGERS

You sure? I don't want to leave you alone.

(SHIRL *has come out of her room and into the lobby. She sits on the sofa.*)

SHIRL

Hi.

ALLY

Hi.

(Finally SIDNEY *comes out of his room and into the lobby. He stops when he sees the two women. Pause.)*

SHIRL

(To SIDNEY*)*

Hi.

SIDNEY

Hi.

SHIRL

Landlord?

(SIDNEY *looks at her for a moment, then goes to* ALLY.)

SIDNEY

(To ALLY, *but really to* SHIRL*)*

Ally, I'm expecting a call from this guy . . . we're supposed to go to Cuba . . . about this proposition . . . so when he calls . . . if he calls . . . tell him . . . I got tied up . . . I won't be able to meet him for dinner . . . something very important came up . . . he'll know what I mean . . . Tell him it's about what we were talking about this afternoon . . . I won't be late . . . tell him I'll call him after supper . . . maybe we still might make it to Cuba . . . Okay?

(SHIRL *is laughing through all this.* MRS. ROGERS *does not see it.)*

ALLY

Who is he? What's his name?

SIDNEY

He knows his name! (*To* MRS. ROGERS) Ready? (*They start out. To* ALLY) What do you say? You happy? (ALLY *nods, very happy indeed*) Good. I want you to be happy.

MRS. ROGERS

Good night, Ally.

ALLY

Good night, Mrs. Rogers. Good night, Pop. (SIDNEY *and* MRS. ROGERS *go out.* SHIRL *and* ALLY *look at each other for a moment. Then she runs upstairs to her room, throws her purse at the wall, collapses on the bed and angrily starts humming the tune of a popular song.* ALLY *has wandered out to the porch. The sound of the purse being thrown breaks his mood and he goes back to his room.* MRS. FESSLER *comes primly down the hall and goes out.* ALLY *turns off the radio, sees the flowers, takes them and goes up to* SHIRL'S *room. Because her door is ajar, he has heard her singing. For a long moment* ALLY *hesitates, trying to decide whether or not to go into* SHIRL'S *room. He finally decides to go in.* SHIRL *looks up, sees who it is, and stops singing, but she makes no move toward him.* ALLY *is tremendously embarrassed now, wondering why he ever did this in the first place*) I just . . . I saw your door open and . . . (*She still doesn't say anything. Just looks at him. He throws the flowers on the bed*) I just wanted to . . . you know. (*She starts singing again, as before.* ALLY *sits down, some distance away from her, and presently he begins singing with her, the two of them singing softly and badly, and on* ALLY'S *part, quite self-consciously, the saccharine lyrics of whatever song is currently popular. When they finish the song, there is a long silence. She takes a flower from the bunch and gives it to* ALLY. *They both laugh.*)

SHIRL

(*Finally*)

You got a quarter?

ALLY

Ma'am?

SHIRL

Can I borrow it a minute?

ALLY

Sure.

(*He gives her one. She takes it, flips it, looks at it, hands it back to him.*)

SHIRL

Thanks. (*Pause*) Get my bill ready, will you? I'm checking out.

ALLY

Where you going?

SHIRL

Fly now—brrruppp!—pay later.

Dimout

In the darkness we hear a radio commercial about borrowing money from a loan company.

Scene 2

Later that night.

MR. GOLDBLATT *is sitting on the roof.* SOPHIE *and* MAX *are on the porch. They are sitting together but obviously not speaking.* ALLY *comes out with two glasses of water. He gives one to each of them, then goes to the lobby for his book, and joins them on the porch and reads. We hear cha-cha music in the distance from a nearby hotel.*

SOPHIE

Thank you. I wonder if they're having dessert yet.

MAX

Look at the ice, Sophie.

SOPHIE

If she started cooking at seven o'clock that means . . . chopped liver takes at least half an hour.

MAX

You see how they make it?

SOPHIE

And the stuffed cabbage. I bet they're having dessert now.

MAX

(*Picking the ice cube out of his glass*)

Look how nice they make it with a hole in the middle. That's very nice. Sophie. You see it? It's just like a regular piece of ice only they put a hole in the middle.

SOPHIE

I'm not speaking to you.

MAX

I called up. What do you want me to do? I told her half a dozen times I apologize.

SOPHIE

Ally, will you tell your Uncle Max I'm not speaking to him any more.

MAX

Look how she tells him tell me. I'm sitting right here. You think I don't hear what you told him tell me?

SOPHIE

What do you think, Ally? You like her?

ALLY

Uh huh.

SOPHIE

The truth?

(ALLY *nods.*)

MAX

A piece of ice. In the whole world a piece of ice is a piece of ice. No. In Miami it's not good enough for them. They got to make it fancy. A hole in the middle like a doughnut. If you want a doughnut, buy a doughnut. You want a piece of ice, how come they got to make it like a doughnut?

SOPHIE

Don't give yourself a heart attack.

MAX

It makes me so mad.

(*At this point* SIDNEY *comes in. He carries a cake, covered with a napkin. He is full of energy.*)

SIDNEY

Hi!

SOPHIE

Sidney! What happened? You had a fight?

SIDNEY

What fight?

MAX

What're you so early?

SIDNEY

I had a wonderful time.

SOPHIE

It's ten o'clock. How can you eat a meal and leave the minute you finish? Max, what time is it? Ten o'clock?

SOPHIE

In the first place, it's not ten o'clock, it's almost eleven, and in the second place, what's it your business in the first place? Look how they watch me like a hawk. Come on, slugger—(*He grabs* ALLY) Get inside there. I got a surprise for you.

(*They all go into the lobby.*)

SOPHIE

Sidney, will you please? Tell us. What happened? Did you like her? You going to see her again? How'd you leave it?

SIDNEY

First I got a surprise. Ally, close your eyes and open your hands. (ALLY *does so*) What's your favorite kind of cake?

ALLY

Coconut.

SIDNEY

Not coconut. Your favorite.

ALLY

That's my favorite.

SIDNEY

All right. Your other favorite.

ALLY

Angel food.

SIDNEY

What're you, trying to be funny? What's your favorite cake?

ALLY

Coconut.

SIDNEY

I'm going to floor you.

ALLY

What do you want me to say?

SIDNEY

(Taking the napkin off the cake)

Honey cake. She asked me what's your favorite, I told her. Honey cake.

ALLY

Where'd you get that idea?

SIDNEY

You ever see a kid in your life? Whatever I do, it's no good.

SOPHIE

She made a cake?

SIDNEY

In two minutes. Go ahead. Take a piece. Just break it off there. I never seen anything like it in my life. In two minutes, she mixed a couple things together, just like that, a cake. I want to tell you, Sophie, that woman is some cook.

SOPHIE

(Tasting the cake)

She likes it very spicy.

SIDNEY

Max?

MAX

Delicious.

SOPHIE

I don't make it quite so spicy.

SIDNEY

(*To* ALLY)

You I'm through with altogether. Coconut.

SOPHIE

But it's very good.

MAX

Delicious.

SIDNEY

Is that delicious? I'm telling you. Sophie, honest to God, for the first time in I don't know how long, I really feel good inside. You know? Proud of myself. You ought to see that room she's got. The whole thing is maybe as big as my car, but the way she's got it fixed up—like a palace.

SOPHIE

I can't tell. Max, does he mean it?

SIDNEY

I should drop dead—

MAX

Now I'm first worried.

SIDNEY

I mean it. Ally can tell. Ally, look in my face. Do I mean it? In my whole life, except for Milly, may she rest in peace, I never met such a wonderful woman.

SOPHIE

(*Hugging* SIDNEY)

Sidney . . . Sidney . . . I'm so happy . . . I don't know what to . . .

(*She is crying.*)

MAX

Good. Now I know she feels all right. You're crying? Good. She don't cry for twenty minutes I know she must be sick.

(SOPHIE *embraces* MAX.)

SIDNEY

I really mean it, Max. This woman is no dummy, and one thing I'm sure about. My son would have a home as good as any kid in this country, and I don't know, a lot of things can happen, but right now, I'll tell you the truth. I'm pretty sure . . . if I take her out a couple more times I'm pretty sure we'll get married.

(*Pause. They are all moved by the occasion, almost to tears. They all hug and kiss each other individually, ending up with* MAX *kissing* SIDNEY *on both cheeks.*)

MAX

(*Crying in spite of himself*)

I'm very happy, Sidney. (*He blows his nose*) I'm proud of you for once in your life.

SIDNEY

(*On the verge of tears*)

What're you crying? Look, Sophie. Look who's crying.

MAX

Crying. All of a sudden I'm crying. Who's crying? (*He takes* ALLY *in his arms*) You're a good boy, Ally.

(*He pinches him.*)

SOPHIE

Sidney . . . I'm so happy . . . Ally . . . (*She takes* ALLY *in her arms*) She'll make you such a home. I know this woman.

SIDNEY

(*To* MAX)

And I'll tell you something else. For the first time in my life, even the idea of having a five-and-ten sounds good to me.

MAX

Sidney, please. Do me a favor. I want you to think very careful first. I know you already a long time. One minute you could love something, the next minute, in the ash can. So you take your time tonight. You think about it. In the morning we'll talk some more.

SOPHIE

Do it, Sidney. Listen to me. You won't be sorry. You'll have a good life. You're not a boy any more. You've got responsibilities.

SIDNEY

I know it, Sophie. I know I have.

MAX

Come. We'll go to bed.

SOPHIE

I know it's very hard for you, but you won't be sorry, I'm sure of it.

MAX

Good night, Sidney.

SOPHIE

Good night, Sidney.

(*She kisses* ALLY, *and then* SOPHIE *and* MAX *go upstairs to their room. There is a long pause.* ALLY *and* SIDNEY *just sit there.*)

SIDNEY

Well? What do you think?

ALLY

I don't know.

SIDNEY

You like her?

ALLY

If you do.

SIDNEY

I'm asking you.

ALLY

Well, she seems very smart and I think she's good-natured.

SIDNEY

She's really crazy about you. That's all she could talk about. I told her wait. She don't know you like I know you. Wait till she finds out what a nag you are.

ALLY

(*Sitting on* SIDNEY'S *knee*)

You know something? When you see a star you make a wish? Well, tonight I saw one coming home from the restaurant, so I wished, even though I don't believe in that stuff—

SIDNEY

Oh, sure—you!

ALLY

—and it looks pretty good so far.

SIDNEY

What do you say. You want a soda?

ALLY

Pop?

SIDNEY

Come on. I'll buy you a soda.

ALLY

Did you really mean that? What you said before?

SIDNEY

What?

ALLY

About getting married.

SIDNEY

Of course I mean it.

ALLY

Because you want to?

SIDNEY

What do you think? I don't want to?

ALLY

You're not doing it just for me.

SIDNEY

Will you stop nagging? Huh? For two minutes?

ALLY

I think it's very important.

SIDNEY

You want a soda or don't you?

ALLY

We've got to talk about it.

SIDNEY

I told you. I like the woman. Now leave me alone about it.

ALLY

I'm very happy about it.

SIDNEY

(*Going behind the desk*)

What happened to that couple supposed to check in we had that reservation?

ALLY

Well, they came but they didn't like the rooms.

(SIDNEY *sees the card turned up signifying* SHIRL'S *check-out. This stops him cold. There is a long pause.*)

SIDNEY

When'd she check out?

ALLY

About seven.

SIDNEY

What'd she say? She say anything?

ALLY

She just checked out.

(SIDNEY *gets out the large transcript sheet, just to be doing something, and goes through the motions of checking it.*)

SIDNEY

You got a mistake here.

ALLY

Where?

SIDNEY

This girl in three-four. What're you carrying her by the day for? She's by the month.

ALLY

I just broke it down that way. She's by the month, but I made it pro rata like we always do.

SIDNEY

If she's by the month I want it by the month.

ALLY

You can't on the transcript. You got to break it down and carry it day by day. That's the way you have to do it.

SIDNEY

What're you, telling me how to run a hotel? Don't tell me transcript. I'm telling you how I want it.

ALLY

You don't really want to marry that woman, do you?

SIDNEY

What're you, starting up again? What do you think's so wonderful about some jerkwater town in the woods there? You forgot already? Nine o'clock they fold up the streets. You want a cup of coffee, you could die first. You think that's such a wonderful life? How could you forget so quick? It's death up there.

(SIDNEY *goes to their room,* ALLY *pursuing him.*)

ALLY

I didn't ask you to. I don't want you to.

SIDNEY

Will you leave me alone?

ALLY

I told you that. Not for me.

SIDNEY

(*Pacing*)

What? What do you want from me? What? All of a sudden you got me . . . I don't know . . . crazy. I will! I told you. Now leave me alone about it. What do they want me to do? Bury myself in a lousy five-and-ten because I've got a kid? What's it a crime I've got a kid, they want to put me in jail some place? What am I supposed to do? Drop dead because I've got a kid?

ALLY

You don't want me, I don't want you either.

SIDNEY

What!

ALLY

Go ahead. Go some place. I don't care. Anywhere you feel like. You're selfish and I don't care what you do!

SIDNEY

What're you . . . fresh kid! You talk to me like that? I'm

your daddy and I want a little respect. If I didn't have you on my neck . . . all of a sudden! . . . (*He smacks* ALLY, *knocking him to the floor. There is a long pause.* ALLY *just looks at him*) Ally? I'm sorry, Ally. I swear to God. Ally, you hurt? Ally?

ALLY

That's okay, Pop.

SIDNEY

I lost my temper. I didn't mean it. I wouldn't hurt you, Ally. You know that. I never hit you in my life.

ALLY

That's okay.

SIDNEY

Come on. You want a soda? I'll buy you a soda.

ALLY

Not right now, Pop. I think I'll go to bed.

(*He goes toward the bedroom.* SIDNEY *stands for a moment.*)

SIDNEY

Ally, what do you say? Let's take a ride. Huh? You feel like a ride?

ALLY

Not right now, Pop.

SIDNEY

I need some air. I don't know.

ALLY

Why don't you take one?

SIDNEY

I think I will. I don't know. I need some air.

ALLY

Good night, Pop.

SIDNEY

Good night, son. I'll see you in the morning.

(ALLY *goes into the bedroom.* SIDNEY *goes out, crumpling* SHIRL's *registration card.*)

Dimout

In the darkness we hear the radio playing. There is a station break announcing the time and weather.

Scene 3

Morning.

SOPHIE, MAX *and* ALLY *are in* SIDNEY'S *room.*

ALLY'S *bag is packed. They are waiting impatiently.*

TINA *is sun-bathing on roof.*

MAX

Look what time it is. Sophie. We'll miss the train.

SOPHIE

So we'll get another train.

MAX

What do you think, they got trains every minute like a subway?

SOPHIE

So we'll get an airplane.

MAX

I told you airplane you told me train.

SOPHIE

Max. Read the paper.

MAX

Where could a man go all night? He leaves a little boy alone like that. That Sidney. That's a Sidney? That's some Sidney.

(*He reads the paper.*)

SOPHIE

We can't just go away. He's got to say good-bye first.

MAX

We'll miss the train.

SOPHIE

Max, why don't you tell Ally about the band?

MAX

What band?

SOPHIE

In the school in our neighborhood they got this band, Ally, and all the boys are in it. One of my boys, your cousin Robert, he used to play the trumpet in the band when he was your age. Max, do we still have that trumpet he used to play?

MAX

If we had it once we still got it.

(ALLY *doesn't answer.*)

SOPHIE

You like dogs, Ally? (ALLY *doesn't answer*) I know a man, a neighbor of ours, who is always having dogs every couple months and he keeps asking me if I want a dog. I'll tell you the truth. I always wanted a dog, but I need an excuse for your Uncle Max. He could understand if a boy wants a dog, but if I told him I want one . . .

MAX

What dog? You want a dog?

SOPHIE

Shhh!

(MAX *goes back to his paper.*)

ALLY

We might as well go, I guess. I'll write him a letter.

SOPHIE

Listen, Ally. I don't want you to go away from here mad at your daddy. He's a little boy, Ally, at forty-two, and you're a man at twelve. But he loves you, Ally. He really loves you and you can't hate the man for that.

ALLY

I'll just make sure I didn't forget anything and then we'd better go.

(*He goes into the bedroom.* SOPHIE *walks over to* MAX *and gives him a look.*)

MAX

What'd I say? You want a dog? I'll buy you a dog.

(SIDNEY *comes around the corner and into the lobby. He stops at the desk.*)

SIDNEY

Frank? (FRANK *is not in sight.* SIDNEY *takes a quick look at the vacancy rack, then goes into his room. To* MAX *and* SOPHIE) What're you doing up so early?

(*They both just look at him.*)

MAX

So where you been?

SIDNEY

When? I just stepped out, two minutes, for a cup of coffee.

MAX

Coffee. A new word for it.

(ALLY *comes into the room. He stops when he sees* SIDNEY. *Pause, then* ALLY *goes to his suitcase, opens it to put in a few books that he forgot.*)

SIDNEY

What're you doing?

MAX

Come on, Sophie. We'll miss the train.

SOPHIE

Shhh! (*To* SIDNEY) Sidney, he made up his mind. He wants to live with us.

SIDNEY

Ally?

MAX

What then? He's going to live here? Where'd you go all night?

SOPHIE

Max. Sit down. (*To* SIDNEY) Let's have a plain talk, Sidney. You met a very nice woman. You want to settle down? Get married? Tell me, Sidney. For once in your life the truth.

SIDNEY

(*A long pause*)

Listen. I want to. I like her. She's a wonderful woman, but, listen, I thought it over; I drove around all night just thinking about it and we're just not right for each other. (*To* ALLY) You know what I mean? I'm not a five-and-ten-cent character. I've got to go for the bundle. I've *got* to. I'd rather go my whole life and never make it than settle now for what . . . peanuts? That's death for me. Ally, don't you understand that? (ALLY *turns away from him*) Listen, Ally. We'll make out here some way. I been down a million times, you know that, but I always bounce back up.

SOPHIE

Max, get a taxi.

MAX

Bounce, bounce. You want to bounce? Bounce. This is a little boy. He's got to have a home.

SIDNEY

Ally?

(MR. GOLDBLATT *enters, walking slowly. As he reaches the porch, he meets* MAX, *who mutters once more "bounce," to* MR. GOLDBLATT'S *amazement.* MR. GOLDBLATT *sits in one of the chairs on the porch.*)

SIDNEY

(*To* ALLY)

You really want to go?

SOPHIE

I'll wait outside.

(*She goes out to the lobby. There is a long pause.*)

SIDNEY

Ally?

ALLY

Well . . . good-bye, Pop.

(*He holds out his hand to shake with* SIDNEY.)

SIDNEY

You mad at me?

ALLY

I'm not mad.

SIDNEY

Then what do you want to go for?

ALLY

. . . You know. If you don't have me to worry about . . . You'll probably have to go on the road and everything.

SIDNEY

I don't know. Maybe they're right. What's the use kidding myself, I'm not going to get that money. I talked to three guys, they laughed at me.

ALLY

You'll have to give Frank two-weeks' notice. And the electric company. You'll have to write them to get the deposit back. You want me to write them for you?

SIDNEY

I look at you and . . . I don't know. Maybe he's right, your

Uncle Max. What have I got? What can I give you? At least with them you'll have a decent home. You'll go to bed on time, and eat on time and . . . I don't know. It's crazy. You know the only man I know who's got it made? Your Uncle Max. He's buried alive, but he's got it made.

ALLY

Mr. Diamond called again. I told him you'd call back.

SIDNEY

Listen. Don't look so miserable. The way I operate, in two minutes, I'm back on Easy Street. I'll look around, get me a real hot line. I can always make a bundle on the road. And listen. You don't like it with Max up there, I'll put you in one of them fancy military schools. Would you like that? You know? With that strap under your chin and everything. How about that? And I'll come see you Christmas or something, we'll go down the street, everybody'll think you're a general or something. Huh? Would you like that, Ally?

(*There is a long, long pause.*)

ALLY

Sure, Pop. (*He holds out his hand*) Well . . . good-bye, Pop. I don't want to keep them waiting.

(*They shake hands, then* ALLY *turns and starts out.*)

SIDNEY

Ally? Ally boy! (ALLY *stops, turns around*) Who knocked out Rudy Zymeck? Newark, 1939.

ALLY

For one million dollars?

SIDNEY

For one million dollars.

ALLY

Alex Luke. Eleven . . . (*Running to* SIDNEY *and hugging him*) Pop! I don't want to go.

SIDNEY

Ally . . .

ALLY

I won't nag you any more and I won't talk back and I'll eat good and . . . Pop . . . Pop . . . I won't get in your way. Let me stay here. Please, Pop.

SIDNEY

Ally . . . Ally boy . . .
(MAX *comes back in.*)

MAX

(*To* SOPHIE)

You ready? (*Goes into* SIDNEY's *room. Sees them in embrace*) Come on, the meter's running.

ALLY

(*Getting up*)

I'm not going.

MAX

What're you, like Sidney already? You're going. You're not going.

SIDNEY

What do you mean, like Sidney already? You trying to poison my kid's mind?

MAX

Sure. You think I want him to grow up a bum like you?

SIDNEY

Bum?

MAX

Bum. Bum. You know it yourself.

SIDNEY

Who's a bum?

MAX

Bum!

ALLY

He's *not* a bum!

SOPHIE

(*Coming in*)

Max!

MAX

Where you been all night? With a tramp some place?

SIDNEY

What's it your business?

SOPHIE

Shhhhh!

SIDNEY

You don't like the way I live?

MAX

Bum.

SIDNEY

I don't like the way *you* live!

SOPHIE

All right. All right a minute. All right!

SIDNEY

Bum.

SOPHIE

Shh! (*To* ALLY) You don't want to go?

ALLY

I won't go. You can't make me.

SOPHIE

Nobody's trying to make you.

SIDNEY

All I did, I asked you one thing. A favor. Loan me a couple dollars. No. You want to take my kid away.

MAX

Loan you? Why should I loan you?

SOPHIE

Max!

MAX

I don't have ice with a hole in the middle. Fancy. Everything fancy. With my money! Sure. Why not? Be fancy. You want a piece of ice, buy a piece of ice. Like everybody else. No. You got to make it fancy with a hole in the middle. And then you come to me? No. No, Sidney. Nothing. Not a penny.

(SOPHIE *turns him around and steers him, like a baby carriage, to the far corner of the room.*)

SIDNEY

Listen, Max. Will you listen? All I need is fifty-three hundred dollars to meet this payment on the rent. Then the pressure's off. You know the deal— Listen. I got all that money up for security. The whole last year's rent in advance. I can't just walk away and leave it.

SOPHIE

Max? . . .

(*She puts her arm around him, as though to lead him off into the corner for a private conversation.*)

MAX

Don't ask me. No. Nothing. Not a penny.

SOPHIE

What can you do? Leave him like that? They'll put him out in the street.

MAX

You know how many garter belts I got to sell to make five thousand dollars?

SIDNEY

Make it three. The owner's a personal friend of mine. I'll give him a few dollars, he'll leave me alone. Listen, Max. If you came to *me* for help . . . After all, you're my brother.

MAX

No more! I'm not your brother.

SOPHIE

Max.

MAX

You want him? Take him. From now on. *She's* your brother.

SIDNEY

(*To* MAX)

Listen, Max. Can you make it two?

SOPHIE

Max. Give him, Max. For the boy. What're you stingy? You're going to live forever? All right. A terrible thing. You'll have two thousand dollars less in your will. Who's it going to cost? Albert?

(*This does it. It stops* MAX *cold, knocking all the wind out of him.*)

MAX

Albert. (MAX *takes out his checkbook*) This is the last time, Sidney. You could crawl on your hands and feet. I'll give you a thousand dollars and that's all. Not a penny more, you could break a leg.

(*He sits on the sofa and starts writing the check.*)

SIDNEY

A thousand? What am I going to do with a thousand?

ALLY

Can't you make it fifteen hundred, Uncle Max? We need five hundred for the laundry bill alone!

(MAX *looks at him, reacting to this.*)

SOPHIE

Max, Please.

(*Resigned, he writes out the check.*)

SIDNEY

Thank you, Max. I appreciate it.

(*He reaches for the check.* MAX *looks at him a moment, then turns away and goes to* ALLY. *He gives the check to* ALLY, *who puts it in his pocket.*)

SOPHIE

(*Kisses* SIDNEY)

Good-bye, Sidney. I hope you get on your feet.

MAX

Come on, Sophie. You'll cry later. The meter's running.

(MAX *and* SIDNEY *go out to the lobby.*)

SOPHIE

Ally? (*She motions for him to come to her. She takes an address book from her purse and copies down a number*) Ally, I'll give you the number. Her telephone. Mrs. Rogers. You know? Who could tell? (*Kisses* ALLY) Good-bye, Ally. Take good care of him.

(*They go to the lobby.* SIDNEY *gets the suitcases and seven candy boxes from behind the desk.* MAX *carefully counts all seven boxes.*)

MAX

You're a good boy, Ally. (*He gives him a pinch*) Ah, Sidney. That's a Sidney in America?

(MAX *and* SOPHIE *go out.*)

ALLY

(*Calling after them*)

Good-bye.

SIDNEY

(*There is a short pause*)

Okay, big shot. Hand it over. (ALLY *hands him the telephone number. As* SIDNEY *looks at the paper with the phone number,* ALLY *takes the check from his side pocket, folds it carefully, several times, then places it in his breast pocket*) Louise Rogers?

What am I supposed to do with this? (ALLY *shrugs*) Give me the check.

ALLY

You want it? Try and get it.

(*He puts up his hands, ready to box.* MRS. FESSLER *comes in, gloriously drunk. She gets her key from the rack and goes through the hall.* SIDNEY *comes at* ALLY, *and they both start laughing and boxing as*

The Curtain Falls